THE
MONEY
MANUAL
1992

PETER PASSELL

A FIRESIDE BOOK
Published by Simon & Schuster
New York   London   Toronto   Sydney   Tokyo   Singapore

Fireside
Simon & Schuster Building
Rockefeller Center
1230 Avenue of the Americas
New York, New York 10020

First Fireside edition 1992

FIRESIDE and colophon are registered
trademarks of Simon & Schuster Inc.

Manufactured in the United States of America

10 9 8 7 6 5 4 3 2 1

Library of Congress Cataloging-in-Publication Data is available

ISBN: 0-671-76112-9

DESIGN: Stanley S. Drate/Folio Graphics Co. Inc.

CONTENTS

Investments at a Glance

	Easy Access Low Penalty	Risk
Bank Money Market Accounts	best	none
Money Market Funds	best	low
Credit Union Deposits	best	none
Tax-Exempt Money Market Funds	best	low
Bank CDs	good	none
U.S. Treasury Bills	good	none
Passbook Savings	best	none
Short-Term Bond Funds	best	low
U.S. Savings Bonds	fair	none
CollegeSure CDs	good	none
Immediate Annuities	poor	low
Common Stocks	fair	med/high
Stock Mutual Funds (Open-End)	good	med/high
Stock Funds (Closed-End)	fair	med/high
Bonds	fair	med/high
Zero-Coupon Bonds	fair	med/high
Bond Mutual Funds	good	med/high
Mortgage-Backed Securities	good	med/high
Tax-Exempt Bonds	fair	med/high
Tax-Exempt Mutual Funds	good	med/high
Tax-Exempt Unit Trusts	good	med/high
Deferred Annuities	fair	low/med
Cash-Value Life Insurance	poor	low/med
Precious Metals	good	med/high
Foreign Currency	good	med/high
Foreign Bond Funds	good	med/high

Likely Return	Tax Shelter	Minimum Investment $	Good for Retirement Account?	See Page
med	none	2,000	yes	5
med	none	1,000	yes	9
med	none	500	yes	8
med	yes	2,000	no	11
med	none	1,000	yes	12
med	some	10,000	yes	15
low	none	100	no	16
med	none	2,000	yes	16
med	some	25	yes	17
med	none	500	no	20
med	some	10,000	no	21
high	some	2,000	yes	24
high	some	1,000	yes	28
high	some	2,000	yes	38
med	none	5,000	yes	41
med	none	2,000	yes	45
med	none	1,000	yes	44
med	none	1,000	yes	48
med	yes	5,000	no	51
med	yes	2,000	no	55
med	yes	2,000	no	54
med/high	some	5,000	yes	58
med	some	5,000	no	62
?	some	1,000	yes	79
?	none	5,000	yes	80
med/high	none	1,000	yes	82

Introduction

Eager to discover the four ways that pyramid power can transform $1,000 into a million in less time than it takes Shirley MacLaine to write a bestseller? How about the top-secret, no-money-down strategy that Donald Trump and the Sultan of Brunei might use to corner the market for office space in downtown Tokyo?

So am I. If you hear from anyone who is ready to spill all, call me collect. . . .

On second thought, don't bother. If you're like me, you're probably fed up with investment guides that promise the moon and the stars for just $19.95 plus sales tax. You've also run out of patience with all those fat, deadly serious treatises on money management that are full of indecipherable graphs and read like bad translations from Serbo-Croatian.

Investing, for those of us who have discovered that once-in-a-lifetime offers come at least once a week, can be a frustrating business. On the one hand, we are pretty sure that well-researched investment strategies can pay off, whether the amount of money in question is $2,000 or $200,000. On the other hand, we have learned the hard way that it is a jungle out there. Half the people who offer financial advice don't know what they are talking about. And most of the ones who really are experts put their own interests ahead of yours, pushing the investment products that pay the highest sales commissions.

That's where *The Money Manual 1992* fits in. It won't help you get rich quick. It won't eliminate the need to make some choices of your own. But it should help you thread your way through the money maze with minimal effort, earning higher returns at lower risk. Best of all, the advice is very specific and up-to-date. *The Money Manual 1992* never tells you to see

1

your local broker or banker: If an investment is worth making, I'll tell you who to call and at what phone number.

Use this book as a reference: The chart on pages iv–v will get you where you need to go in a matter of seconds. Descriptions of investment options are short and to the point, meant for busy people who have more enjoyable ways to pass the time than taking care of their money. Or, if you have a minute, browse the big ideas on the next few pages. They may make your life as a part-time investor a bit easier, and perhaps even a little richer.

Unsolicited investment advice is bad investment advice.

At this very minute, hundreds of "account executives" working for brokerage houses with fancy-sounding names you've never heard before are phoning prospective clients. Some are perfectly respectable—the modern equivalent of the clean-cut young men who used to work their way through college selling chrome-plated vacuum cleaners and leather-bound encyclopedias that no one really needed. Some are crooks, looking for suckers to buy rare coins at 20 times their market value or stocks in companies that specialize in recovering platinum from moonbeams.

Don't even try to figure out who's which. When you hear that friendly, confident voice on the other end of the line, hang up.

The investment that did wonders for your buddy Harry in the comptroller's office won't necessarily work for you.

No investment is perfect for everyone. The go-go mutual fund that makes sense for a happy-go-lucky bachelor with a good job could be pure poison for a couple approaching retirement with only Social Security and a small nest egg to fall back on. The municipal bond that doubles the after-tax return for a successful neurosurgeon in Boston could be a costly mistake for a schoolteacher in low-tax Florida.

Let Harry figure out what's best for Harry. Match your investments to your own tax situation, your ability to bear losses, and your need for ready access to the cash.

When in doubt, diversify, diversify, diversify.

Some people think that the smartest investors in 1955 were the ones who put their entire life savings in a little-known company called Polaroid. But they weren't the smartest, just the luckiest. With hindsight, it is always easy to figure the best investment strategy. The trick is figuring it out before the fact.

2

And for most people, most of the time it pays to divide money among a variety of investments.

There's more to diversification than the homily about not putting all your eggs in one basket. For one thing, merely mixing investments may not help to reduce risk: Buying $5,000 worth of five separate mutual funds that invest in government bonds may be no better than putting the whole $25,000 in a single mutual fund because all government bond funds tend to go up and down together with changes in interest rates.

Economists have something subtler—indeed, almost magical—in mind when they speak of the advantages of true diversification. By mixing your investments cleverly, you can sometimes improve the trade-off between risk of loss and expected return. For example, putting some of your money in foreign stocks may allow you to earn roughly the same overall return with substantially less chance of losing, say, more than 10 percent of your nest egg in a really bad year.

The best mix of securities is hard to figure; business schools hand out Ph.D.'s to the people who do the figuring. However, research by a Chicago investment company called Ibbotson Associates shows that even a simple blending can make a big difference.

From 1970 through 1989 a portfolio of the largest 500 stocks generated an average return of 11.5 percent a year, almost identical to the average return on an even mix of U. S. stocks, foreign stocks, bonds, money market funds, and real estate. But in four of the 20 years, the all-stock portfolio lost money, and in one year (1974) it fell a whopping 26 percent. The mixed portfolio, by contrast, had only two losing years and the biggest one-year loss was 7 percent.

Too much attention to investments is worse than too little.

In his heart of hearts, every investor knows that he could have made a lot of money if he had only taken a few chances and put a lot more time and energy into the game. Now there's usually nothing wrong with harboring fantasies of opportunities passed by—in my own, I can't quite forget the gorgeous little office building with the big mortgage in downtown Manhattan that was for sale for just $100,000 in 1975.

The trouble comes when fantasies lead to temptation. Unless you are very, very serious about investing and ready to lose a lot of money, avoid the complicated and the exotic. The investments outlined in this short book cover most of the ground that small investors can safely navigate.

3

SAFETY FIRST
Investments That Absolutely, Positively Cannot Turn Sour

Every investor needs a place to keep the money he or she cannot afford to lose. Happily, there are plenty of such refuges from the financial storm, and some of them even pay a decent return.

Nobody wrote the rules on how much of your money should be parked in these supersafe assets. Much depends on your responsibilities and the size of the cushion you need for emergencies. An unmarried 28-year-old with disability insurance and a secure, good-paying job hardly needs more than a few thousand dollars to cover next month's bills. A parent of newborn twins, by contrast, would do well to amass a hefty sum before turning to higher-risk, higher-yielding investments. Consider the following options.

Money Market Accounts from Banks and S&Ls

Money market accounts are checking accounts that pay interest on the cash balance. Checks written on MM accounts can be used to ransom the kids' braces or buy a VCR or anything else you might wish to do with an ordinary check.

Banks are legally permitted to pay as much or as little interest as they please, and to change the rate weekly. Some choose not to pay competitive rates, gambling that depositors won't notice. And some pay high "teaser" rates for a few months to attract new money. Typically, though, banks pay as little as they can get away with in a competitive market—and that usually amounts to a percentage point or two less than the rate on very safe, but less convenient investments like Treasury bills and money market funds (see below).

All bank and savings and loan money market accounts are insured to $100,000 by a government-run agency. *Should your bank go belly-up—a common occurrence these days—Congress is formally pledged to cover any losses to depositors.* If your bank is closed by federal insurers, the money will either be promptly returned or redeposited in another insured bank.

The $100,000 guarantee, incidentally, is good for every insured institution with which you do business. If, for example, you had $300,000 looking for a safe home, the deposit could be fully insured by splitting it into three accounts at three different banks.

If bank money market accounts are as good as checking accounts and pay interest, why would anyone bother with an ordinary checking account? Banks typically put restrictions on money market accounts that make it impractical to use them for day-to-day checking. Some, for example, permit you to write only a limited number of free checks each month. Some set a minimum on money market checks—say, $100. And almost all levy stiff penalties on accounts that fall below a specified minimum balance.

In some cases, banks offer attractive terms to investors who are prepared to open both a money market account and a checking account. Fees on the regular checking account may, for example, be waived as long as you keep some minimum balance ($3,000? $5,000?) in the money market account. And some banks offer package deals, linking a no-fee money market account to an overall commitment to do a minimum amount of business each year with the bank.

For many investors, though, the best strategy for choosing a money market account is the most straightforward: Set up a checking account at a local bank with the lowest fees, most reliable service, and most convenient automatic teller machines. Then shop around for the highest money market yield from a bank or savings and loan that does not unduly restrict access to your money. *There is no reason not to set up an MM account in an out-of-town bank as long as you have easy access to cash in a local checking account*—indeed, money market banking at long distance can be a convenience because checks written on a distant bank take longer to clear. That gives you a few day's more interest on the cash.

To find the banks paying the highest money market rates in the country, check the weekly listings in most big-city newspapers. If your paper doesn't carry them, buy a copy of *The New York Times* (Sunday Business section) or *Barron's,* a weekly financial tabloid. Better yet, check *Money* magazine's "Money Scorecard."

Money magazine's listings can be a little dated because they are published just once a month. But they do include a uniquely useful statistic: the number of weeks over the last six months in which each listed bank has paid exceptionally high rates. Stick with these steady performers: There is no point, after all, in setting up an account only to discover that the interest rate has fallen sharply a month later.

The banks and savings and loans below have consistently paid high money market rates:

	Minimum Deposit for Highest Rates
Custom Savings Maryland 301-486-5200	$ 2,500
First Deposit National New Hampshire 800-821-9049	$ 5,000
Washington Federal Savings District of Columbia 800-537-8744	$ 2,500
Key Bank USA New York 800-872-5553	$ 2,500

Note: Some banks compound interest monthly, crediting your interest income 12 times a year. Others compound weekly or daily or even continuously (if you're curious what continuous compounding could possibly mean, ask a college math major). The more frequently the interest is compounded, the more money you will earn. To compare returns from MM accounts with different compounding policies, ask each bank for the "effective annual yield," or check the table on page 14.

RATING YOUR BANK

Will your bank or savings and loan bite the dust this year? It should not much matter to most depositors because the U. S. government insures accounts to $100,000. Nonetheless, it can be more than a little disconcerting to have your bank or savings and loan shot out from under you.

Those who don't want to risk the experience do have a way of checking on a bank's financial soundness before plunking down their cash. Veribanc, an industry rating firm, ranks banks and S&Ls from no stars to three. The no-star variety is probably insolvent and in the process of being sold or closed by federal insurers. The three-star banks, by contrast, have a big cushion of capital and are very unlikely to fail anytime soon.

Money magazine's monthly lists of banks offering the highest-yield MM accounts and CDs include the rating. So, too, does the Sunday Business section of *The New York Times.* And for a modest fee ($10, chargeable to VISA or MasterCard) Veribanc provides its rating of any other bank that interests you. Phone 800-442-2657.

Credit Union Deposits

Credit unions, which began as savings cooperatives for moderate-income workers whose dimes and dollars were not welcome at commercial banks, now largely duplicate the functions of banks and savings and loans. They offer a variety of interest-bearing accounts, including money market accounts with check-writing privileges. In many cases, interest offered on these accounts is competitive. Moreover, credit union members often have access to personal loans at rates below those demanded by banks.

If the credit union where you work offers competitive money market rates and first-class service, why not bank there? No reason, save perhaps one: deposit insurance.

Deposits in virtually all credit unions are insured to $100,000. But some only carry private insurance to see depositors through a crisis. That may prove sufficient, but it seems pointless to take the chance. *Before plunking down your first dime, check to make sure your credit union is federally insured.* Federal insurance represents total protection on accounts of less than $100,000. No one has lost money in a federally insured credit union, and Congress is pledged to make sure that no one ever will.

Money Market Funds

Money market funds are privately owned mutual funds that invest in U. S. Treasury bills, plus other short-term securities issued by giant banks and corporations. Like bank MM accounts, MM funds permit you to withdraw money quickly and conveniently by writing checks. Like bank money market accounts, funds generally have restrictions on both the number of checks that can be written each month and the minimum size of each check.

But money market shares are not quite the same as bank money market deposits. On the plus side, fund shares represent ownership: If the return on the fund's investment rises, you automatically get the income. On the minus side, the U. S. government does not insure your cash balance: If the banks and corporations that borrow from the fund fail to pay, you bear the loss. *Money market funds typically compensate shareholders for the added risk by paying a percentage point more interest than banks.* Is that enough?

Probably, because the assets of money market funds are very secure. No money fund shareholder—and there are millions—has ever lost a penny. But the first disquieting signs of vulnerability in the business are beginning to show. In the last two years, two corporations have defaulted on big loans (the jargon is "commercial paper") from money market funds. In both cases, the investment companies that manage the funds have shielded shareholders from any loss by making up the difference from their own pockets.

As a matter of self-interest, managers will probably continue to absorb any minor losses incurred by their money market funds. No fund sponsor wants to be known as the first to pay less than 100 cents on the dollar to its money market clients. The unanswered question, though, is, What would happen if the economy went into a tailspin and loan defaults to money market funds amounted to billions rather than millions?

The most conservative investors may wish to avoid money market funds altogether. Bank money market accounts pay less, but there is no way to lose money in one. Other investors should, at the very least, pay attention to where money market funds put their money. U. S. government securities are safest, followed by high-grade loans to banks, followed by loans to corporations—so-called "commercial paper."

Each month *Money* magazine lists the money market funds with the highest yields. However, the following funds are all pretty good bets because they are well managed and keep expenses to a minimum.

	Minimum Investment
Alger Money Market 800-992-3863	$ 1,000
Dreyfus Worldwide Dollar Fund 800-782-6620	$ 2,500
Fidelity Spartan Money Market ($2 fee per check) 800-544-8888	$20,000
Kemper Money Market 800-621-1048 312-781-1121	$ 1,000
Vanguard Money Market Reserves 800-662-7447	$ 3,000

U. S. Government MM Funds

The next best thing to federal insurance on the account is a federal guarantee on the assets that back the account. These funds invest only in U. S. Treasury bills and other federally guaranteed short-term securities. Note, by the way, that you pay a small price for the extra safety—to be specific, about three-tenths of a percentage point in annual yield. But those who live in high-tax states may actually come out ahead in after-tax yield: Most of the income from these funds is exempt from state and local tax.

	Minimum Investment
Benham Government Agency 800-472-3389	$ 1,000
Dreyfus 100% U. S. Treasury 800-782-6620	$ 2,500
Fidelity Spartan U. S. Treasury 800-544-8888	$20,000
Fidelity Spartan U. S. Government ($2 charge per check) 800-544-8888	$20,000

Tax-Exempt MM Funds

Some money market funds buy only short-term securities issued by state and local authorities. The big advantage: The interest income is exempt from federal tax. That doesn't necessarily make them a great investment, however, because they pay less interest than taxable funds. *In fact, the only people who are likely to do better in a tax-exempt fund are those in the highest (33 percent) federal bracket.*

	Minimum Investment
Calvert Tax Free Reserves 800-368-2748	$2,000
Evergreen Tax Exempt 800-235-0064	$2,000
USAA Tax Exempt 800-531-8181	$3,000

Specialized Tax-Exempt MM Funds

The income from some tax-exempt MM funds is doubly exempt for some investors because the funds buy tax-exempt securities issued in a single state. For example, California residents who buy a specialized California tax-exempt fund pay neither federal nor state tax. These double tax-exempt funds pay even less interest, however, than more broadly based tax-exempt funds, and thus only make sense for residents of high-tax states who are in the highest federal tax bracket.

	State Funds Available
Alliance Fund Services 800-227-4618	CA, NY
Dreyfus Service Corp. 800-782-6620	CA, CT, NJ, NY
Fidelity Distributors Corp. 800-544-8888	CA, MA, NJ, NY, PA
T. Rowe Price Associates 800-638-5660	CA, NY
Putnam Financial Services 800-225-1581 617-292-1000	CA, NY

Bank Certificates of Deposit (CDs)

The certificate of deposit is the safest, simplest, and, not surprisingly, the most popular way to store surplus cash for six months or more.

A CD is nothing more than a savings contract between you and a bank or savings and loan. They agree to pay a specified interest rate on a deposit—typically, $1,000 or more. You agree to leave the money on deposit for the full term. With small deposits (say, $5,000 or less) and relatively short periods (say, a year or less) the interest is credited to your account when the CD matures. With larger deposits the interest is usually credited monthly to a separate money market account, or is paid by check.

The longer you agree to leave the money on deposit, the higher the interest rate. Interest on six-month CDs is typically about the same as is paid on money market funds, while the rate on longer-term CDs is usually about a percentage point more than you could earn on U. S. Treasury securities of the same maturity.

Banks are generally willing to give you back your full deposit before a CD matures. But it doesn't make sense to lock money into a CD that you expect to need: The contract with the bank will always specify an interest penalty that sharply reduces the yield on cash that is prematurely withdrawn. One way to have your cake and eat it too, is to buy a handful of CDs with the same maturity—say, four one-year CDs of $5,000 each, rather than one $20,000 CD. That way, if you need some of the cash eight or nine months later, you will not be penalized for prematurely withdrawing the full $20,000.

These days, of course, banks and savings and loans are dropping dead like peonies in a hailstorm. And it is entirely possible that the bank with your deposit will be one of the hundreds to fail over the next few years. But from the depositor's perspective, that is no big deal. All deposits in banks and savings and loans are federally insured to $100,000. You cannot—repeat *cannot*—lose any principal or interest owed.

In some cases, federal insurers notify you that your bank is being closed and mail you a check a few days later. In others, the deposit is automatically moved to another insured bank that has agreed to take over the business of the failed institution. *The only real risk to the depositor, then, is that he or she will lose out on a good deal.* If, for example, you buy a five-year CD paying 10 percent interest and the bank fails in the second year, you probably won't be able to find another bank to match the 10 percent yield. Note, by the way, that institutions agreeing to take over the deposits of the failed banks are not obliged to match the interest return on the CD. If they won't, however, they are obliged to return your money without exacting an interest penalty.

How to choose a CD? It pays to see what sort of package deal you can make with a local bank. Some will throw in free

---

WHEN A CD IS NOT A CD . . .

"Invest as little as $100," trumpets the promotional flyer. "Earn as much as 12.4 percent on 'Money Market Thrift Certificates' . . . No fees or service charges . . . Statements are issued monthly . . . IRA and Keogh accounts are available . . ."

Is it the real thing? Not exactly. The interest rate is real and the corporation issuing the certificates probably has every intention of meeting its obligations to investors who mail in their checks. What is not quite on the up-and-up, however, is the way the deal is packaged. The borrower is not a bank or a savings and loan, and the "money market thrift certificates" are not federally insured, nor are they backed by the rock-solid assets of a money market mutual fund.

In this particular case, the cash is invested in business equipment—everything from airplanes to computers—that is leased to commercial users. Lenders (depositors) to the leasing corporation are merely the firm's creditors: Were it to go bankrupt, owners of the "thrift certificates" could lose part, or even all, of their money.

That does not mean, of course, that uninsured savings certificates issued by a leasing company—or, just as commonly and even more confusingly, by bank holding corporations seeking to increase their capital—are necessarily bad investments. The extra interest may compensate investors for taking the extra risk.

But deciding whether such risks are worth taking is a tricky business, one better left to the MBAs paid by insurance companies and mutual funds to judge creditworthiness of corporate borrowers. It seems particularly problematic to bet on a borrower who coaxes cash from people who think they are depositing money in a bank account. Financial institutions that can offer their customers federal deposit insurance are never coy about it. If the big print doesn't say federally insured, dollars to doughnuts it isn't.

13

checking, free VISA and MasterCard, and a discount on the regular mortgage rate. But people with substantial amounts of cash to deposit—$20,000 or more—can generally do better by shopping for the highest rates. That often means depositing money in another state, where the competition is greatest. But as long as the bank or S&L is federally insured, where you put your money should make no practical difference.

To find the banks and S&Ls paying the highest rates, check the weekly listings in most large-circulation newspapers. The Sunday *New York Times* (Business section) and *Barron's*, a weekly financial tabloid sold at big newsstands, are also reliable sources.

Some CDs compound interest quarterly. Other banks credit your CD account on a weekly or daily basis. The more frequent the compounding, the more interest you will get on your interest. What counts for purposes of comparison shopping is the "effective annual yield." If your bank doesn't advertise this figure, use Table 1 below to get a rough idea of what you may be missing.

TABLE 1

Effective Annual Yields

	A CD paying this rate					
Compounded	6%	7%	8%	9%	10%	11%
	has an effective annual yield of					
Annually	6.00	7.00	8.00	9.00	10.00	11.00
Quarterly	6.14	7.19	8.24	9.31	10.38	11.46
Monthly	6.17	7.23	8.30	9.38	10.47	11.57
Daily	6.18	7.25	8.33	9.42	10.52	11.63

The following banks all have excellent financial ratings and are thus unlikely to fail. Nonetheless, they have been paying very high yields on CDs in recent months.

	Minimum Deposit
Beach Savings (California) 800-232-9200	$2,500
Citibank (South Dakota) 800-248-4669 X-371	$2,500

14

Colonial National (Delaware) 800-441-7306	$1,000
First Trade Union Savings (Massachusetts) 800-242-0272	$ 500
La Salle Bank (Illinois) 312-880-1505	$2,500
New South Federal Savings (Alabama) 800-366-3030	$1,000

U. S. Treasury Bills

Bonds issued by the U. S. government that have maturities of less than one year are called Treasury "bills." They are, of course, guaranteed by the "full faith and credit" of the U. S. government. But they come in minimum $5,000 units and pay about 1 percentage point less than the highest-yielding bank CDs of comparable maturity. Just to confuse matters, they are sold in discount form: You pay less than the face value and receive the full amount when the security matures. The difference is the interest.

Less interest, more hassle . . . why would anyone bother? *The interest on T-bills (as they are known in the trade) is exempt from state and local income taxes.* For high-income residents of high-tax states like California, New York, and Wisconsin, that is the equivalent of about a half-percentage point boost to the rate. Moreover, unlike CDs, T-bills can be sold before maturity without any interest penalty.

For most investors that isn't enough to make up for the greater convenience of a bank CD. But investors seeking an ultrasafe, short-term parking space for a lot of money—say, the down payment on a house—T-bills aren't a bad way to go. Banks and securities brokers will buy T-bills on your behalf for a modest commission. Or, if you have a lot of time on your hands, you can avoid the commission by purchasing T-bills directly from the Bureau of the Public Debt.

For the Federal Reserve's pamphlet "Basic Information on Treasury Bills," write to the Federal Reserve Bank of New York, 33 Liberty St., New York, NY 10045. Information on the latest T-bill offerings can be had from the government's automated phone line. From a touch-tone phone, call 202-287-4113.

Passbook Savings

Back when bankers wore three-piece suits and kept bankers' hours, "savings" meant passbook savings—that's right, the savings registered in those little soft-cover books you kept at the bottom of the sock drawer. Bankers now dress to look friendly and many stay late to accommodate the after-work crowd. But the passbooks and the no-minimum-balance accounts they represented are still around.

Many banks, particularly those outside large cities, offer savings accounts that permit you to earn 4 or 5 percent interest on just a few hundred dollars, and to withdraw small sums on demand without penalty. There's nothing wrong with such accounts. Indeed, there's something right: Kids can use them to learn about thrift and money. The catch is that some people—lots of people over age 60—store large amounts of money in them when they could be earning far more in equally safe, equally accessible accounts.

If you or a loved one have $1,000 or more in an account paying less than 6 percent interest, transfer it to a CD or an insured money market account; let someone else subsidize the banks' stockholders. This seems so obvious a point that it isn't worth making. But at last count more than $100 billion dollars was languishing in low-interest savings accounts across the country.

Short-Term Bond Funds

Mutual funds that invest in bonds generally earn 2 or 3 percentage points more interest than money market funds. But the price of the extra interest earned on long-term fixed-income securities is the risk that the mutual fund shares will decline in value as interest rates in the economy rise.

Short-term bond funds are a compromise between regular bond funds and money market funds. By investing in securities due to mature within a few years, they earn a bit more interest than money market funds while incurring only modest additional risk of fluctuation in share value. With these funds, even a sharp increase in rates—2 or 3 percentage points over a period of a few months—would cost you only a percent or two of your principal. To encourage investors to think of them as substitutes for money market accounts, short-term funds usually permit limited free checking.

The following no-load funds invest in high-grade securities and deduct relatively small amounts for expenses.

	Minimum Investment
Dreyfus Short-Intermediate Government 800-782-6620	$2,500
Scudder Short-Term Bond 800-225-2470	$1,000
Vanguard Fixed Income—Short Term 800-662-7447	$3,000

Tax-Exempt Short-Term Bond Funds

These funds use a similar strategy to increase yields without adding much risk. The difference is that they invest only in tax-exempt bonds, making the income free of federal (but not state) taxes. Note there is no free lunch here: Yields are considerably lower than on the funds above. But they may make sense for investors in the highest (33 percent) tax bracket.

	Minimum Investment
Dreyfus Short-Intermediate—Tax Exempt 800-782-6620	$2,500
USAA Short-Term 800-531-8181	$3,000
Vanguard Municipal Bond—Short Term 800-662-7447	$3,000

U. S. Savings Bonds

Not so long ago, U. S. savings bonds were a national scandal and an insult to small investors. Peddled to people with little knowledge about investments, savings bonds were nothing more than a handy way for Washington to borrow money at below-market rates from the Americans who could least afford to subsidize the Treasury.

All that has changed. Savings bonds are still convenient to purchase and totally safe. But now they also pay competitive rates of interest. Better still, they offer significant tax breaks to everyone and a genuine tax windfall to middle-income investors who use the proceeds to finance their kids' higher education.

Series EE bonds come in denominations from $50 to $10,000. Since the purchase price is half the face value—a hangover from the days when bonds had fixed yields and fixed maturity dates—it's possible to buy one for as little as $25. Most banks sell them in a variety of denominations, charging no commission. Most large employers let you buy them as a payroll deduction. And Uncle Sam even sells them by mail: Write to the Bureau of Public Debt, Parkersburg, West Virginia 26106.

Once purchased, series EE savings bonds cannot be cashed for six months; thereafter, they can be redeemed at any bank. But to receive the maximum interest rate, bonds must be held a full five years. *It thus makes sense to buy savings bonds in relatively small denominations—say, five bonds of $1,000 rather than a single $5,000 bond.* That way, if you need part of the money before the five years is up, you won't pay the interest penalty on the full amount.

Series EE bonds held for five years or more accumulate interest equal to 85 percent of the rate on regular, marketable Treasury securities with a five-year maturity. The interest is paid only when the bond is redeemed, but the interest rate is adjusted every six months (May 1 and November 1). If, for example, the five-year Treasury rate were 8 percent on November 1, 1992, you would receive credit for 6.9 percent interest through the following April. But no matter how low the five-year rate fell thereafter, you would be guaranteed a minimum of 6 percent.

EE savings bonds accumulate interest for up to 30 years. You never pay state or local tax on the income, and you pay no federal tax until you redeem the bonds. That, by the way, is another reason to buy bonds in bite-size multiples: Otherwise you'll pay tax on the full amount even if you need to redeem only a portion.

If you don't want to pay the tax even after 30 years, you can exchange the matured series EE bonds for something called series HH bonds. They yield a fairly miserable 6 percent interest (paid semiannually). But an exchange might still make sense if you expected to be in a much lower tax bracket a few years down the road and wanted to defer the tax liability a while longer.

Just how good a deal series EE bonds are depends on who you are, as well as when and how you expect to use the proceeds. They make no sense for people who expect to spend the money in less than five years—a federally insured bank CD held for two or three years is just as safe, just as easy to cash in a pinch, and will almost certainly pay more interest. Nor do they make much sense for investors who are eager to earn the high returns generated in good years by stocks, and are prepared to take some risk.

But savings bonds are a fine set-it-and-forget-it investment for people who don't want to take chances with their nest eggs, and do covet the inflation protection that comes with frequent adjustment of the interest return. And the good deal looks even better for investors who are eager to avoid the bite of state and local income taxes.

The biggest winners from savings bonds are middle-income parents with young children who want to begin saving for the kids' college expenses. If you qualify for the tax break and follow all the rules, interest income from series EE bonds will be exempt from federal tax.

To qualify, the bonds must be registered in your name (not junior's) and they must have been purchased after December 31, 1989—the bonds Grandma gave you the day you graduated from junior high don't qualify. Second, your income in the year you cash the bonds must not exceed limits set by Congress.

Single parents with adjusted gross incomes under $40,000 and married couples with incomes under $60,000 get the full tax benefit. Single parents making $40,000 to $55,000 get a partial tax benefit; likewise, couples making $60,000 to $90,000. The benefit is proportional to how close you are to the limit: A couple making $75,000, halfway between $60,000 and $90,000, would pay taxes on half the income from the bonds they redeemed.

These income limits, by the way, are indexed to the cost of living, with 1990 as the base year for the calculation. If, for example, prices have doubled by the time little Sharon is ready for Oregon State, the income cutoff for full benefits for her (two-parent) family would be $120,000.

One more important point: Interest from the bonds counts as part of income in the calculation of eligibility for tax benefits. For example, a single parent earning $39,000 would lose part of the tax break if he or she spent more than $1,000 in series EE savings bond interest on tuition in one year.

Sound complicated? It is. Many parents won't know whether they will be eligible for the tax breaks 10 years down the road because they won't be able to predict their income. But it may well be worth taking the chance. Series EE bonds are, after all, a decent enough investment even without the tax break. If college savings is your main reason for considering series EE bonds, before you buy compare them to tax-exempt "baccalaureate bonds" (page 47) and CollegeSure CDs (below).

CollegeSure CDs

Problem: You know you have to start saving now to send Jennifer (age four) to Harvard or Berkeley or Tulane in the year 2005. But since you don't have a fix on what tuition will run, you can hardly begin to guess how much savings will be enough.

One solution: The CollegeSure CD, a federally insured bank CD whose interest rate is tied to an index of college cost inflation. If you deposit money today, you'll know precisely how many years' worth of college the money will cover 6 or 16 years down the road.

Here's how the CollegeSure CD, an investment product sold only by the College Savings Bank in Princeton, New Jersey, works. Each July, the nonprofit organization that administers the College Board entrance exams computes the average annual cost of tuition and living expenses at 500 colleges. In 1989–90, for example, the figure was $13,256, up from $12,205 the year before.

Based on these figures, the College Savings Bank will sell you a CD today whose redemption value is a predetermined chunk of whatever the College Board says the typical college will cost in the year of your choice. For example, the price in 1990 of one year's worth of college starting in the year 2005 was $16,335.

Actually, the College Savings Bank doesn't insist that you spend it on tuition: If 18-year-old Jennifer decides to forsake higher education and follow her guru to Nepal, the proceeds of the matured CD are still paid out in cash. Indeed, like other bank CDs, it is possible to cash a CollegeSure CD whenever you please, provided you pay a penalty for premature liquidation of the account.

The interest credited to the CD each year is figured as 1 percentage point less than the rate of inflation in college costs for CDs of $10,000, and 1.5 percentage points less on smaller amounts. If, for example, you invested $10,000 and college costs rose 12 percent next year, you would be credited with 11 percent interest. Under no circumstances, though, can the annual yield fall below 4 percent.

Are CollegeSure CDs a good deal? Yes and no. In ordinary times you could expect to earn a bit more interest by investing in the highest-yielding federally insured CD you can find (see previous page), and rolling over the proceeds once a year. But that is not an entirely fair comparison.

A strategy of buying and rolling over short-term CDs does offer some protection against general increases in prices in the economy. But only the CollegeSure CD is locked into the cost index for colleges. Think of CollegeSure, then, as a combination of bank CD and inflation insurance. *If peace of mind is your number-one goal, it is probably the best way to save for college.* For details, including computerized savings plans tailored to your specific requirements, call the College Savings Bank at 800-888-2723.

If, on the other hand, you are willing to put up with a modest amount of inflation risk in exchange for the prospect of a better return on your savings, consider ordinary CDs. And don't forget the other ways to accumulate cash for college. If you expect your family income to remain below $60,000, consider the special tax advantages offered by series EE U. S. savings bonds (see page 19). And if you are willing to gamble that inflation rates will remain moderate, buy tax-exempt zero-coupon bonds (see page 45) or U.S. Treasury strips (page 46).

Immediate Annuities

Say you are 65 years old and have $200,000 in savings to spend in retirement, plus Social Security. You could be conservative and use no more each month than the interest on the $200,000. But that would mean you would leave the planet with $200,000 in the bank, unspent. Or you could take a chance, assuming you would live for perhaps 20 years more, and spend down the principal accordingly. But what if you were lucky enough—or unlucky enough—to live longer?

Life insurance companies have no better idea how long you'll live than you do. But they do know that, on average, a 65-year-old male will live 15 more years. And by playing the averages, they can afford to sell you a guaranteed monthly income for the rest of your life. The product, called an "immediate" annuity to distinguish it from a popular tax-sheltered investment misleadingly called a "deferred" annuity, is available from more than 100 life insurance companies.

You put down, say, $200,000. And (if you happen to be age 65) the insurer guarantees to pay as much as $2,100 a month for the rest of your life. If you are younger than 65 or are female the payout is smaller because your life expectancy is longer. If you want to guarantee continuing payments to a surviving spouse, the insurer will pay you 5 to 10 percent less each month, depending on your spouse's age.

Some points to think about:

• Flat monthly payments make no allowance for inflation. And chances are, the cost of living will be far higher 10 or 20 years down the road. Thus an annuity can't guarantee a constant standard of living. *Only Social Security and government pensions are fully protected against inflation erosion.*

• Annuities offer a modest tax break. The portion of the monthly payment that the IRS deems a return on principal is not taxed. To calculate the tax break, ask the IRS for publication 575. Or buy a copy of *J. K. Lasser's Your Income Tax,* which includes the updated tables.

• If your insurance company goes bankrupt, you may lose part of your annuity. To minimize that small risk, buy an annuity only from a company with an A+ rating from A. M. Best, an insurance company rating service. The company selling the annuity can provide this information.

Better yet, once you choose an insurance company, purchase an analysis of its financial strength from one of the insurance company ratings services. A. M. Best sells "Best's Advanced Company Report" for $15. Phone 908-439-2200 for details. Weiss Research offers a similar product for $25. Phone 800-289-9222.

• Some employers permit retirees to take their pensions as lump sums. If yours is one of them, compare the monthly pension to which you are entitled with the best immediate annuity available for the same money. A "rollover" of the funds can usually be accomplished without incurring tax liability. It's worth remembering, by the way, that private pensions are guaranteed by a federal agency; annuities are not.

• The monthly return offered by insurance companies varies by as much as one-third. These all have top credit ratings and currently pay top rates:

Federated Life, Owatonna, MN
Great American Life, Los Angeles
Sun Life of Canada, Toronto
Nationwide Life, Columbus, OH

But the only way to find the very best annuity is to shop around. For an up-to-date list of companies and annuity terms, call U. S. Annuities at 800-872-6684. Their publication, *The Annuity Shopper,* costs $10.

2

RIDING THE WEALTH CURVE
... WITH SEAT BELTS ON
Calculated Risks for
Exceptional Gains

Bank CDs and U.S. Treasury Securities are great for sleeping at night. But almost every investor hopes to make a bit more than the risk-free return available from government-guaranteed securities. And unless you are an exceptionally light sleeper, there is no reason why you shouldn't venture a step or two into the domain of higher risks and higher returns.

The key is keeping your feet on the ground. Just because your brother-in-law made $6,000 overnight betting on a little company that perfected the no-fat potato chip doesn't mean you will be as lucky. And just because the stock market has been going up for six straight weeks (or months or years) doesn't mean that it won't go down once you've placed your bet.

Smart investors avoid the big plunge, trying instead to capture an extra 3 or 4 percentage points' return each year while bearing little added risk. That may not sound like much, perhaps. But it could mean the difference between tuition at Harvard and tuition at the state teachers' college for little Angela. Or it could make it possible to spend two weeks in Europe next summer rather than two weeks at the same old cottage at the lake.

Common Stocks

Common stocks represent tiny ownership slices of large corporations. If, for example, the Amalgamated Flavoring and Insecticide Company has 10 million shares outstanding, the owner of a single share has a legal claim on one ten-millionth of the company's assets and income—and, in most cases, has one vote out of 10 million in choosing the company's directors.

Once issued by the corporation, most stocks are traded in organized markets (like the New York Stock Exchange), or through a computer network called the "over-the-counter" market. Exchanges, operating under a combination of their own rules plus Washington's, afford small investors some protection against fraud. Just as important, they increase the liquidity of fractional ownership in companies; shares in large corporations can usually be sold on a few minutes' notice.

AmFlav stock is selling for $61 a share. Is it a good buy? Economists will tell you the underlying value of a stock is the sum of expected earnings per share in future years—or, alternatively, the value of the company's assets, were they to be sold.

That may well be correct. But, in the short run (and as John Maynard Keynes said, in the long run we are all dead), stocks are worth whatever the highest bidder will pay. Indeed, a winning strategy in stock picking is to find companies that, for one reason or another, are out of favor for no good reason and wait for their reputations to improve.

For most people, most of the time, stocks have proved a worthy investment. Just $1,000 invested in a basket of the 500 largest stocks in 1946 would have been worth $135,000 by the end of 1989. *And at no time in the last century has an investor patient enough to hold stocks for 10 full years actually lost money.*

But the story of stocks doesn't always have a happy ending. First, the market sometimes takes sickening dives: No investor can forget that belly-wrenching week in October 1987, when the average stock lost one-third of its value. Many who lost their nerve and sold near the bottom have yet to recoup their principal.

Second, the average performance of stocks conceals a mix of big winners and big losers. Investors who buy the stocks of just a few different companies have sometimes suffered losses in the best of times. Third, the calculations showing average returns of 17 percent or more over the last decade assume that the investor bought and held his shares. However, with the encouragement of their brokers, most buy and sell frequently. And just two "round-trips" a year typically slices 5 percent off an investor's earnings.

Should you put some money into stocks? It makes sense for most middle-income investors, the ones willing to bear some risk in order to have a chance at the historically superior earnings from stocks.

Should you pick stocks on your own? Probably not. Individual investors pay relatively high commissions to buy and sell shares in small quantities. Moreover, few individuals are prepared to sink enough capital into stocks to diversify their holdings. That's why *The Money Manual 1992* recommends mutual funds as the way to go (see page 28). If, however, you believe you can beat the market alone, or if you simply want to invest in stocks for the fun and diversion of it, consider the following advice.

First, use discount brokers to save money on commissions. For specifics, see below. Second, buy some independent advice on which stocks are worth owning. No recommendations are infallible. But the Value Line Investment Survey does have a long history of beating the averages: If you had invested $10,000 on their advice in 1965, buying and selling as they suggested along the way, you would have ended up with $1.8 million by 1990. Moreover, Value Line's weekly offering is packed with statistical information needed to evaluate the prospects of individual companies on your own.

Purchased by the year, Value Line is quite pricey. But a trial 10-week subscription, which includes an up-to-date report on some 1,700 stocks, is available for $65. Yes, they do take plastic.

The Value Line Investment Survey
711 Third Avenue
New York, NY 10017
800-833-0046

Third, join the American Association of Individual Investors. The AAII's newsletter is packed with very sophisticated analyses of stock-picking strategies. And meetings of local chapters feature first-rate speakers.

American Association of Individual Investors
625 North Michigan Avenue
Chicago, IL 60611
Annual fee: $49 (includes a copy of the AAII's mutual fund guide)

When Your Broker Wears a Black Hat

Veteran investors learn (sometimes the hard way) that the brokerage business is a tough business. Invariably, the investment products that sell are the ones that are sold most aggressively. And the most successful securities salesmen are often the ones with the least interest in the welfare of their clients.

That does not mean, of course, that successful account executives are all crooks. But it does mean that the incentives to cut corners at the clients' expense are almost always there. And as a practical matter, the small investor's only real defense against brokers' shady tactics is the vigilance of the brokerage house.

How to tell which brokerage houses police the behavior of their brokers, and which turn a blind eye? Diana Henriques, a star reporter for *The New York Times,* combed the complaint files of the securities industry trade associations to rate each brokerage house by the number of disciplinary cases reported over the decade of the 1980s divided by the number of brokers they employ.

As Ms. Henriques notes, the rating system is not perfect. Minor infractions such as sloppy record-keeping are lumped together with felonies like stealing cash from customers' accounts. Moreover, some firms may be better or worse than the ratings suggest because they have changed policy in recent years. For that matter, a firm with a spotless record through 1988 may have changed its stripes by now.

Still, the list is worth a close look. At the very least it pays to ask a few questions before doing business with a broker who scores badly in Ms. Henriques's ratings.

Brokers with No Violations
Legg Mason
Robert W. Baird
Fidelity Brokerage

Brokers with Less Than 1% Violations
Robinson-Humphrey
Bateman Eichler
Piper, Jaffray
A. G. Edwards
Merrill Lynch
First of Michigan

Brokers with 1 to 2% Violations
Alex Brown
Janney Montgomery
Dean Witter
Shearson
Thompson McKinnon
Advest
Paine Webber
Prescott, Ball

Brokers with 2 to 4% Violations
Cowen
Oppenheimer
Prudential-Bache
Smith Barney
Kidder, Peabody
Tucker, Anthony
Dain Bosworth
Stifel, Nicholaus
J. C. Bradford
J. J. B. Hilliard
Wheat, First
Interstate/Johnson Lane
Morgan Keegan

Brokers with 4 to 7% Violations
Raymond James
Gruntal
Bear, Stearns
Edward D. Jones
Blunt, Ellis

Choosing a Broker

Brokers come in three price classes. The "full-service" type offers virtually every sort of investment product under the sun and will happily provide advice on which ones are right for you. The catch is they charge premium fees to buy and sell securities.

On second thought, make that catch*es:* The advice full-service brokers provide is typically less than unbiased. Account executives make bigger commissions on some investments than on others. And while few are inclined to sell you products that are utterly unsuited to your needs, fewer still are about to reduce their own living standards in order to increase your income or security.

Worse yet, they have a vested interest in keeping your money moving from investment to investment because every transaction generates a commission. Sometimes it actually does pay to buy and sell stocks quickly. More often, though, it makes sense to buy securities for the long haul, and few full-service brokers are inclined to make that easy.

Brand-name discount brokers like Charles Schwab (800-654-3321) and FidelityPlus Brokerage (800-544-7272) don't provide much personal service; the voice on the other end of the line won't remember the birthday of your spouse or the name of your dog. But brand-name discounters generally do sell a wide range of products, and they typically charge just half as much as full-service brokers to buy or sell a few hundred shares of stock. Best of all, they don't provide much advice.

Deep-discount brokerage houses, by contrast, sell a more limited range of financial products; some do nothing more than buy and sell stocks. And they never offer assistance in deciding what to buy or when. But buying and selling is done through the same automated systems used by full-service brokers. Like other brokerage houses, accounts are insured against embezzlement and bankruptcy by the Securities Investor Protection Corp. (up to $500,000). And here's the really good news: They charge just one-quarter the full-service rates.

Mercer and Company, a consumer analysis service, publishes a survey of the fees charged by 175 discount brokers, listing rates for each on 25 hypothetical transactions. You can buy a copy of the survey for $29.95 (write Mercer and Co., 80 Fifth Avenue, New York, NY 10011, phone 800-348-7583). Or you can simply use one of these, the cheapest deep-discount brokers included in the survey:

K. Aufhauser, Plainview, New York	800-645-9486
Muriel Siebert, New York	800-872-0711
First National Brokerage, Omaha	800-228-3011
Pace Securities, New York	800-221-1660
Pacific Brokerage, Los Angeles	800-421-8395 213-939-1100
St. Louis Discount	314-721-7400

Stock Mutual Funds (Open-End)

Mutual funds are private, for-profit corporations that pool the money of thousands of individual investors and invest it in securities. As with other corporations, your share in the profits (or losses) is proportional to your holdings. But mutual funds differ from other corporations in that you can always cash in your shares for their market value. If, for example, you own one-millionth of a mutual fund whose stock portfolio has a market value of $2 billion, you can sell your shares back to the fund for $2,000. All it takes is a phone call.

Why are mutual funds the better way to buy stocks? They burn less of your money on transactions and administration. The typical fund charges 1 to 2 percent annually for all services rendered, and some charge much less (see the section on Index Funds on page 34). Second, they offer an investor with just a few thousand dollars the opportunity to diversify into hundreds of different stocks. Third, they offer expertise. That is no guarantee of success, of course. But it sure beats the advice offered by most brokers. And quarterly reports make it easy to keep track of successes and failures.

Deciding that the mutual fund route is the way to go is only the first step. The next is choosing the fund or funds that are right for you. About half of the more than 1,000 funds available can be eliminated because they charge hefty fees up front to buy them. While some so-called load funds have excellent performance records—the Fidelity Magellan Fund, for example—so, too, do many "no-load" funds. And there isn't a reason in the world to believe that the 2 to 8 percent fee you pay a salesman on day one is buying you anything that can't be had for free.

By the same logic, it makes sense to avoid funds that have relatively high operating expenses. Most of what you are paying for is high salaries, high profits, and a high turnover of securities, none of which correlates with bottom-line success in making money for you.

But some choices are not so obvious. Mutual funds are usually classified by their investment strategies. Which is best for you depends on your taste for risk—more important, on your willingness to bear losses in hard times. Consider the many options shown below.

Growth Funds

These are the classic mutual funds, the ones that push for maximum gains and are willing to take some lumps in the process. *All the funds on this short list have done exceptionally well when the market was going up, while protecting shareholders from the full brunt of a down market.* Remem-

HIDING THE LOAD

Once upon a time it was easy: Some mutual funds charged up-front sales fees or "loads" of as much as 8.5 percent. Others charged no sales fee, and were thus known as "no-load" funds. The managers of the no-load funds made their profit on the annual fees they charged for investment advice and overhead.

Brokerage houses, to no one's surprise, liked "load" funds—indeed, with the exception of money market funds, where competition for customers was fiercest, brokers only sold funds with loads. Consumer-minded advisers, by contrast, preferred the no-load funds. Why pay a fat sales fee to a middleman, they asked, when no-load funds of equal quality could be purchased direct from the management?

But as the cost of advertising and operating mutual funds rose, managers sought new ways to increase their revenue without imposing up-front sales charges. And under pressure from the industry, government regulators agreed in 1980 to let them levy an annual fee to offset the cost of ongoing sales and promotion. Today, half of all mutual funds charge these so-called 12b-1 fees, generating an extra $1 billion annually for the mutual fund industry.

The 12b-1 fees, regulators rationalized, would serve the interests of both shareholders and managers by allowing funds to grow rapidly and thereby spread their overhead costs over a larger base of customers. But, according to a recent study commissioned by the Securities and Exchange Commission, it hasn't worked out that way. Funds with annual 12b-1 fees—the average fee is about 1 percent of fund assets—have not grown any faster than the industry average. Moreover, funds with these hidden loads generally have higher average expenses and lower after-expense returns for investors.

The moral: Avoid funds with up-front or hidden loads unless there is no comparable fund to buy with a decent track record. Once you've invested in a fund, keep a careful watch on the fund's ratio of total expenses to assets. As a benchmark, remember that the expenses of typical diversified stock funds run to about 1.3 percent of assets. Taxable bond funds average about 1.0 percent. Money market funds rarely deduct more than 0.7 percent.

Want to know just how bad the fees can get? Contemplate this short role of dishonor culled from a variety of fund categories. Many of these funds, by the way, also charged fees to buy or redeem shares.

	Total Expenses 1990 (percent of assets)
Drayfus Strategic Aggressive	3.06
Keystone International	2.92
MFS Lifetime Emerging Growth	2.82
MFS Lifetime Global Equity	3.05
Prudential-Bache Global Genesis	3.27
Prudential-Bache Global Natural Resources	3.07

ber, though, past performance is an uncertain predictor of future performance. Growth funds are not for folks who will need every penny next year to cover Dad's nursing home costs or make a down payment on a condo.

	Minimum Investment
IAI Regional 800-927-3863 612-371-2884	$ 5,000
Janus 800-525-3713	$ 1,000
Mutual Beacon 800-553-3014	$ 1,000
Twentieth Century Growth 800-345-2021 816-531-5575	none
Gabelli Asset 800-422-3554	$25,000

Balanced Funds

These funds are less aggressive in seeking gains than the growth funds, at least in theory putting investors at less risk. In practice, though, it doesn't always work out that way. The funds listed below should offer a measure of protection when the market goes bump in the night.

	Minimum Investment
Dodge and Cox Balanced 415-434-0311	$1,000
Founders Blue Chip 800-525-2440	$1,000
Safeco Equity 800-426-6730 206-545-5530	$1,000
Scudder Growth and Income 800-225-2470 617-439-4640	$1,000
IAI Stock 612-371-2884	$5,000

Financial Industrial Income $ 250
800-525-8085
303-779-1233

All-Weather Funds

Eager to cash in on the superior long-term returns investors
have traditionally earned from common stock, but desperately
afraid of losing your shirt in an October 1987–style market
collapse?

One way to limit the risks is to limit the percentage of your
nest egg that is committed to stocks. You might, for example,
invest just 20 percent of your money in the stock market,
keeping the rest in a mix of CDs, money market funds, and
perhaps even precious metals. That way, a 30 percent fall in
stock prices would mean just a 6 percent fall in the overall
value of your portfolio.

Another way is to invest in "all-weather" mutual funds—
funds that limit risk by investing in stocks that fluctuate less
than the average or by mixing stock with investments in bonds
and money market securities. *There's no free lunch here:
Conservative all-weather funds will go down less than the
stock market in hard times, but will go up less in good times.*
Still, they do represent one way to dip a toe into the market
without getting really wet.

	Minimum Investment
Blanchard Strategic Growth 800-922-7771 212-779-7979	$ 3,000
Clipper Fund 800-776-5033 213-278-5033	$25,000
Vanguard STAR 800-662-7447 800-362-0530 (PA only)	$ 500
Vanguard Wellesley Income Fund 800-662-7447 800-362-0539 (PA only)	$ 3,000

Small-Company Funds

Almost every big company started as a small company. And the best way to make a killing in the stock market is to find the next Xerox or the next Apple before they become the next Xerox or the next Apple.

Well, that's the idea anyway. Funds that specialize in smaller-capitalization stocks have not done very well in the last few years; few have outperformed the Standard and Poor's index of the largest 500 corporations. But the past is not a very good predictor of the future. And, for what it's worth, all of these funds are widely recognized as well managed.

	Minimum Investment
Founders Discovery Fund 800-525-2440	$1,000
Janus Venture 800-525-3713	$1,000
Nicholas II 414-272-6133	$1,000
New Beginning Growth 800-332-5580	$2,000
Twentieth Century Ultra 800-345-2021	none

Sector Funds

Most investors buy mutual funds in search of broad diversification. Suppose, though, you have a hunch that energy-related stocks are going to go up in the next few years, but don't want to bet on the management of any single energy producer. You might do well to buy a mutual fund that specializes in energy stocks. The funds below haven't necessarily performed exceptionally in recent years. Most, moreover, levy sales charges and have relatively high operating expenses. But they do offer one-stop shopping in a variety of sectors.

	Load	Phone
Century Shares (Financial)	none	800-321-1928 617-482-3060

	Load	*Phone*
Fidelity Select Portfolios	3.75 percent	800-544-6666
Biotechnology		617-523-1919
Energy Services		
Leisure		
Chemicals		
Environmental Sciences		
Telecommunications		
Utilities		
Financial Strategic Health Service	none	800-525-8085
		303-779-1233
National Aviation & Technology	4.75 percent	800-654-0001
		212-482-8100
Vanguard Specialized Energy	1 percent	800-662-7447
		215-648-6000
Vanguard Specialized Health Care	1 percent	800-662-7447
		215-648-6000

Note: Sector funds specializing in gold and precious metals are listed on pages 79–80.

Index Funds

Can fund managers beat the stock market averages? At first take, the question seems silly. If they can't, why were they paid an average of $362,000 in 1989 for trying?

In fact, many common stock funds do very, very well for a few months or a few years. And a few have done superbly over much longer periods—Fidelity Magellan (800-544-6666) and the Guardian Park Avenue Fund (800-221-3253) are standouts. But a surprisingly large number have actually done worse than the proverbial monkey that picks investments by throwing darts at the stock listings in *The Wall Street Journal*. *Over the last decade fewer than half of all diversified stock funds have outpaced the Standard and Poor's index of the largest 500 listed stocks.* And since 1969 the typical stock fund has returned one-fifth less to investors than a random investment in the S&P 500.

Look closely, and it's not hard to see why. Apart from a few dollars a week for bananas and flea powder, monkeys don't cost much to keep in the stock-picking business. Mutual fund managers, by contrast, on average charge 1.7 percent of assets for research, advertising, and expense-account limos—sometimes much more (see page 30). Inevitably, this money comes off the investors' bottom line.

What's more, the typical stock fund must hold 5 to 10 percent of its assets in money market securities in order to meet the unpredictable demands of owners, who have the right to liquidate their shares on a day's notice. These cash assets do earn some interest, of course. But the return is far less than the average double-digit returns from the stock market over the last decade, and thus represents a drag on earnings.

That's why some institutions (pension funds, college endowments, bank trust departments) long ago gave up trying to beat the averages and now merely try to match them. They buy "index funds"—mutual funds that invest in hundreds of stocks in proportion to their size.

If, for example, the total value of General Snacks and Toxic Waste Disposal Inc. represents two-tenths of one percent of the value of all 500 stocks in the Standard and Poor's index, a fund that is tracking the S&P 500 will automatically invest 20 cents out of every $100 in GenSnack stock. When the market goes up, index funds go up in lockstep. Of course, when stocks fall, so too do the index funds. But once the computer programs are written, investing an index fund's money requires little human intervention. Index funds are thus able to make a profit charging their customers less than 1 percent in fees annually.

Most stock index funds are geared for institutional investors, and, in order to minimize expenses, insist on very large minimum investments—$100,000 or more. But a handful are now available to the general investing public.

	Minimum Investment
Vanguard Index Trust—500 Portfolio (tracks the S&P 500 index) 800-662-7447 800-362-0530 (PA only)	$ 3,000
Dreyfus Peoples Index Fund (tracks the S&P 500 index; 1 percent redemption fee) 800-782-6620	$ 2,500

	Minimum *Investment*
Fidelity U.S. Equity Index 800-544-8888	$10,000
Vanguard Index Trust—Extended Market (includes smaller stocks) 800-662-7447 800-362-7447	$ 3,000

International Funds

Until the 1980s, "the stock market" was shorthand for U. S. stocks—shares trading on the New York, American, and over-the-counter exchanges. No more. The booming markets in Asia and Europe have whetted the appetite of investors who previously thought that Canadian paper mill stocks were pretty exotic buys. And now, it is hard to find an investment company or brokerage house that isn't peddling a mutual fund that specializes in foreign equities.

Are international funds, which invest in stocks from many different countries, right for you? Paradoxically, the reason most people invested abroad in the 1980s is the wrong reason to invest abroad in the 1990s. *The spectacular run-up in stock prices that made foreign stocks in general (and Japanese stocks, in particular) so popular is unlikely to be repeated.* Indeed, some analysts believe that a recession or a reversal of the maniacal boom in real estate prices in Japan could lead to a sharp stock price decline.

But there are still reasons to invest (with caution) in foreign stocks. First, they offer an opportunity for diversification, for reducing risk without reducing the likely return on your over-all investment portfolio. Second, they provide a relatively cheap and easy way to hedge against a decline in the value of the dollar. If, for example, the Japanese yen were to appreci-ate by, say, 25 percent, the dollar value of holdings in Japanese stocks would appreciate with it.

The funds listed below were selected from the dozens available because they do not levy up-front sales charges and do keep expenses relatively low.

	Minimum Investment
Ivy International 800-235-3322 617-749-1416	$1,000
T. Rowe Price International Stock 800-638-5660 301-547-2000	$2,500
Scudder International Fund 800-225-2470 617-439-4640	$1,000
Vanguard Trustees' Commingled-International 800-662-7447 800-362-0530 (PA only)	$3,000
Vanguard International Equity Index (This is a true index fund [see page 34], designed to track the Morgan Stanley Capital International Index.) 800-662-7447 800-362-0530 (PA only)	$3,000

DOING WELL BY DOING GOOD

Would you like to make money on your investments, but not at the price of supporting the arms race or destroying the rain forest or manufacturing cigarettes? A number of mutual funds now promise to invest only in socially responsible companies. What's more, a few of them are managing to do reasonably well by doing good, last year outpacing the performance of the average mutual fund.

Some mild warnings. One fund's views on social responsibility may not mesh with your own. Not everyone who believes that it is wrong to invest in the tobacco industry also believes that it is wrong to invest in the oil companies that operate the Alaska pipeline. Not everyone who opposes investments in South Africa believes it is wrong to buy the stock of American companies that fight to keep out unions. Read the fund's prospectus before you plunk down your hard-earned bucks.

Then there is the matter of just how well you really will do in the long term by investing responsibly. Do-good funds made money in 1990 by avoiding defense contractors and by betting on companies in the anti-pollution business. They did not do as well in 1991.

The range of potential investments that meet most people's definition of social responsibility is certainly large enough to permit a competitive return. Amy Domini, a market analyst, claims to have assembled a group of 400 socially responsible companies whose stocks collectively outperformed the stock market as a whole for 19 quarters out of 20. However, the long-term track record of the older mutual funds in the do-good group is not reassuring: On balance, they have lagged the return on the market.

If you do want to give socially responsible investing a whirl, consider one of the following:

	Minimum Investment	Sales Charge
Calvert SIF Growth 800-368-2748 301-951-4820	$1,000	4.75
Calvert Ariel Appreciation 800-368-2748 301-951-4820	$2,000	4.75
Dreyfus Third Century 800-782-6620	$2,500	none
Pax World Fund 800-767-1729	$ 250	none
Parnassus 800-999-3505	$2,000	3.5
Working Assets (Money Market Fund) 800-533-3863 415-989-3200	$1,000	none

Closed-End Stock Funds

With an ordinary "open-end" fund—the great majority of the funds in business—shareholders have the right to sell their shares back to the fund on a day's notice. With a "closed-end" fund, the managers make no such promise. The only way to sell is to find someone else willing to buy.

That restriction sounds more limiting than it actually is. Shares in closed-end funds are freely traded on the stock exchanges, and it is hardly ever difficult to find buyers for a few hundred or a few thousand shares. Still, why bother when a no-load, open-end fund with a similar objective and investment strategy can be found?

One answer is that some closed-end funds are unique. One type of fund, the sort that invests in the stocks of a single foreign country, is only available in closed-end form (see page 40). But there are other good reasons to prefer closed-end funds to their open-ended cousins.

38

Open-end funds are prisoners of market fads. When stock prices are low, they are rarely able to scoop up bargains because no money is available: In lean times investors are generally cashing in more fund shares than they are buying. But when the stock market is booming, investors generally flood the funds with cash, leaving fund managers with the unpleasant choice of buying overpriced stocks or holding the money in low-yield money market securities. That is why the most successful open-end funds are sometimes driven to suspend sales of new shares.

The managers of closed-end funds, by contrast, are under no such pressures. They must, of course, satisfy stockholder-elected boards of directors that they are doing their jobs. *But they can, and often do, ignore market fashions to pursue long-term investment goals.*

Benjamin Graham, the guru of investing by the fundamentals, had an even better reason for looking first to closed-end funds. The shares of many funds, he noted, traded for less than the underlying value of the stocks they owned. Thus a fund might own $50 million worth of stock, yet trade on the exchanges for just $40 million—a 20 percent discount from net asset value. Discovering which closed-end funds sell for a discount is a snap: The financial section of every big-city newspaper publishes a table each week with closed-end share prices and the value of the assets each share represents.

When funds sell for a discount, owners are ahead of the game in three ways. First, they earn a bonus on regular dividends. If, for example, the stocks a fund owns are, on average, paying a 4 percent dividend, fund owners who acquire shares at a 20 percent discount enjoy the equivalent of a 5 percent yield. Second, funds trading at a discount often appreciate very rapidly during stock market booms as trendy investors rush to cash in on the anomaly of the discount—and, in the process, close the gap. Third, the managers of closed-end funds that chronically trade at a discount are often pressed to liquidate the assets and pay off the shareholders in cash. When they do, those who bought shares at a discount enjoy a windfall profit.

Not every closed-end fund trades at a discount, of course. Indeed, the trendiest funds, the new ones specializing in stocks from a single country, often sell at enormous premiums over their asset value (see page 40). But the funds in the short list on the next page, all diversified stock funds, typically have sold at a discount.

Adams Express
Baker Fentress
Central Securities
Gambelli Equity
General American Investors
Growth Stock Outlook
Liberty All-Star Equity
Niagara Share
Royce Value Trust
Salomon Brothers
Source Capital
Tri-Continental
Zweig Total Return

AN OPEN-END FUND FOR CLOSED-END FUNDS

Wall Street is full of bright, ambitious MBAs looking for yet another way to coax fees from investors. The latest is an open-end fund that specializes in the shares of closed-end funds selling for substantial discounts from their net asset value. The Franklin Balance Sheet Investment Fund is, in essence, betting that a diversified portfolio of these funds will do better than the stock market averages.

For reasons explained above, that isn't a bad bet. But before you plunk down your hard-earned dollars (the minimum initial investment is $10,000, or $1,000 for a retirement plan), think carefully. The fund is brand new, and thus has no track record to use for comparison with other funds. The sponsor, the Franklin fund group, charges a 1.5 percent load, plus another 1.5 percent to redeem shares held less than one year. It's worth noting, too, that the managers are not limiting themselves to running a fund of funds. Franklin plans to use some of the money to buy stocks that are out of favor or selling below book value—a strategy that sounds promising, but is hardly original and hardly guarantees success.

Still, the Franklin Balance Sheet Investment Fund does offer a no-fuss, no-muss way to diversify among closed-end holdings. For a prospectus, call 800-342-5236.

Country Funds

Funds that specialize in stocks from a single country are all the rage these days—probably because the first ones did so well. On the plus side, they offer the only practical way to invest in small-country stocks. On the minus side, they are immensely volatile: Buy them only if you have a stomach for the roller coaster.

All are closed-end funds, with fixed numbers of shares that are traded on exchanges rather than bought and sold from the fund management. Some currently sell at enormous premiums to their net asset value—to put it another way, you may end up paying $1 for 60 cents worth of stock. Here's the latest list of country funds. By the time this book reaches you, there will no doubt be a few more to choose from. Anyone game to invest in Liberia?

First Australia Prime Fund	Malaysia Fund
Austria Fund	Mexico Fund
Brazil Fund	First Philippine Fund
Chile Fund	Portugal Fund
Germany Fund	Spain Fund
New Germany Fund	First Iberian Fund
Swiss Helvetia Fund	Taiwan Fund
India Growth Fund	ROC Taiwan Fund
Italy Fund	Thai Fund
Korea Fund	United Kingdom Fund

P.S.: A somewhat safer and perhaps more rational way to bet on the new markets is to buy the closed-end fund that buys stocks in them all: The Templeton Emerging Markets Fund, which has recently been selling at a discount from its net asset value.

Fixed-Income Securities

Common stockholders are, for better or worse, in business. When their company does well, they do well; when it doesn't, they don't. Those who buy fixed-income securities—bonds, mortgage-backed securities, leases—are creditors: The fine print on the contract specifies that they must be paid first in both good times and bad.

That makes fixed-income securities seem safer than stocks, and sometimes they do prove safer. *But novice investors often neglect the largest source of risk in owning fixed-income securities, the risk associated with unpredictable changes in interest rates.*

An example should help. (Pay attention, folks, the money you save will surely be your own.)

Suppose Exxon sells bonds in $1,000 chunks, promising to pay 10 percent interest ($100) each year for 20 years and then return the principal. At the time the bonds are offered, 10 percent interest from a giant oil company with rock-solid credit seems like a pretty good deal, and investors scoop them up at the $1,000 price that Exxon is asking. But a few years later inflation kicks up in the economy, and the interest that banks and other lenders charge goes up to match. When Exxon decides to sell more bonds, the company finds that it must offer 15 percent interest ($150 a year) in order to persuade investors to buy them.

Nothing has happened to Exxon's credit—no one doubts its ability to meet its financial obligations. But investors trying to find a buyer for one of Exxon's old 10 percent bonds will discover that the most anyone will pay is about $800—a $200 capital loss. Why, after all, pay full price for a bond yielding $100 a year when it is possible to purchase another Exxon bond with roughly the same maturity that yields $150?

Now, such "market risk" is a two-way street: If interest rates fall in the economy, the 10 percent Exxon bonds will be worth more than $1,000. But the rules of the game are clear: When you buy a tradable fixed-income security that matures many years in the future, you are, in effect, betting that interest rates will not go up very much. That may be a risk worth taking, but it is not a risk that can be ignored. Moreover, with most fixed-income securities, it is a greater source of price volatility than the risk that the debtor will default.

Does that mean conservative investors shouldn't ever buy long-term fixed-income securities? Not necessarily. But they aren't recommended for people who might need their cash back in a hurry. And, like stocks, they should never be more than a part of a diversified portfolio of securities. Here is more specific information needed to make sensible choices.

Government Bonds

First things first. The biggest seller of bonds—and the world's largest debtor—is the U. S. Treasury. Unlike corporate bond issuers, there is no chance the government will default on its obligation. Nor is there any chance that the government will seize the opportunity created by falling interest rates to refund your principal prematurely and reborrow the money at lower cost. For unlike the bonds of corporations, Treasury bonds do not contain "call" provisions that permit advance repayments at the expense of lenders.

Treasury bonds are easy to buy and sell in $10,000 chunks; they are available through most brokers for commissions that are generally far lower than the commissions on stock purchases. The interest on Treasury securities (but not income from selling them for a profit) is exempt from state and local income tax. But (surprise!) the price of this exceptional liquidity, partial tax exemption, and zero risk of default is a lower interest rate.

Corporate and Agency Bonds

Those who crave a higher return may be tempted by long-term corporate bonds. Many issuers (the regional Bell telephone companies, for example) have credit that is almost as good as Uncle Sam's and pay about a half-percentage point more interest.

Another way to take home a bit more interest is to buy "agency" bonds—bonds issued by federal agencies that are not formally guaranteed by the U. S. Congress, but are backed implicitly by Washington. One example is the debt of the government's Financing Corporation (FICO), which is selling billions of dollars worth of bonds to cover the costs of closing insolvent savings and loans. Interest on FICO bonds happens to be exempt from state and local taxes. But the return on many agency bonds is not: Look before you leap. Remember, too, that agency bonds are not as liquid as U. S. Treasury issues and you thus might lose an extra $10 per $1,000 face value if you are in a hurry to sell.

Junk Bonds

The way to earn much, much more interest is to buy bonds issued by corporations that cannot convince the bond-rating companies they are very likely to repay their debts. Now everyone who knows a little bit about so-called junk bonds knows that they are at best a bad deal and, at worst, a fraud and a scam. But in this case, a little knowledge can be misleading.

Junk bonds—salesmen prefer to call them "high-yield" bonds—are indeed riskier than so-called investment-grade bonds. *But for hardy investors, the sort who sleep well in foxholes, the extra 3 to 8 percentage points interest can more than compensate for the greater probability of default.* The one sort to avoid under almost every circumstance is the "payment-in-kind" (PIK) bond, where interest consists of a promise to pay back more than the initial principal when the bond matures. Most PIK bonds, alas, have been issued by deeply indebted companies that have not the faintest idea how they will honor the pledge.

Few small investors have the expertise to find the swans

among the geese; fewer still have sufficient cash for adequate diversification in corporate bonds. Bond ratings, plus the basic information that brokers can provide about individual issues, are just not sufficient to make good choices. And even as much as $50,000 is inadequate to build a well-diversified portfolio of debt securities.

That is why it generally makes sense to buy bonds through mutual funds. The funds below have relatively good track records and relatively low operating costs. They are all no-load funds—nobody gets a sales commission. Remember, however, even the best fund managers cannot fully protect you from the risks associated with interest rate fluctuations.

Babson Bond Trust—Long-Term Portfolio
800-422-2166
816-471-5200

Dreyfus A Bond Plus
800-782-6620

Fidelity Government Securities
800-544-6666
617-570-7000

Fidelity High Income
(junk portfolio)
800-544-6666
617-570-7000

T. Rowe Price High Yield Bond
(junk portfolio)
800-638-5660
301-547-2000

Vanguard Fixed Income—Investment Grade
800-662-7447
800-362-0530 (PA only)

Vanguard Fixed Income—High Yield
(junk portfolio)
800-662-7447
800-362-0530 (PA only)

Zero-Coupon Bonds

Who would buy a bond that pays not a cent of interest for 10 or 20 years? Lots of people, it turns out. For the accumulated interest on zero-coupon bonds (the Internal Revenue Service calls them "original issue discount" bonds) is paid in full when the bond matures and the principal is repaid.

Here's how they work. You lend a corporation (or a government or a bank), say, $1,720. Twenty years later, the borrower gives you back $10,000—which in this case is the equivalent of 9 percent interest (including interest on the unpaid interest) for the 20-year period.

If turning $1,720 into $10,000—a six-fold increase in just 20 years—sounds like a heck of a deal to you, join the crowd. Ever since they were invented a decade ago, Wall Street has been churning out zero-coupon securities by the billions for clients ranging from the ITT corporation to the U. S. Treasury to the State of Michigan. But before you get carried away, consider the pros and cons.

TABLE 2 ═══════════════════════════════════

Zero-Coupon Yields

and matures in this many years	If the bond earns this much interest				
	7%	8%	9%	10%	11%
	you must invest this much to end up with $1,000				
10	$503	$456	$415	$377	$343
15	356	308	267	231	201
20	253	208	172	142	117
30	127	95	71	54	40

A zero-coupon bond provides no current income. But unlike an ordinary bond that does deliver cash twice a year, a "zero" implicitly guarantees that you will be able to reinvest the interest earnings at a rate specified on day one. *Thus if you believe that interest rates are headed down, a zero-coupon bond gives you the double whammy of today's rates on the principal and today's rates on future earnings.*

By the same token, the penalty for guessing wrong about future interest rates is magnified. And the risk that interest rates will rise, the bane of all long-term fixed-rate investments, is greater.

There are other drawbacks as well. With an ordinary bond, you get regular interest checks. So if a borrower goes belly-up after 10 years, you've at least gotten some of your money back. With zeros, all interest payments are postponed, and if the borrower goes bankrupt in the nineteenth year, you may never see a penny returned on the bond. Not surprisingly, those who buy zeros are especially fussy about the creditworthiness of the bond issuers.

With an ordinary bond, you pay income tax on the interest as you collect the money. With a zero-coupon bond there is no interest payment, but there is tax due on the interest that has accrued on your behalf. Eventually, you get all your money. But eventually can be a long, long time, during which you are obliged to shell out hefty sums in taxes. This explains why most zero-coupon securities are either tax-exempt bonds issued by state and local authorities, or taxable bonds purchased for tax-deferred accounts—Keogh retirement plans and the like.

Are zero-coupon bonds right for you? Only if you are prepared to make a bet about future interest rates, and then only if you have some specific financial goal in mind. State governments, for example, are issuing "baccalaureate bonds"—tax-exempt zero-coupon bonds that mature when your child is ready to go to college (see box on the next page).

Remember, too, that zero-coupon buyers pay a penalty for the convenience of knowing just how much cash they will end up with. The implicit yields on zeros are generally a half-percentage point lower than the yields on ordinary bonds of equivalent risk and maturity.

Brokers who sell tax-exempt bonds will always be able to find some zero-coupon versions for you. And any dealer in Treasury bonds will be able to drum up a Treasury version.

In fact, Uncle Sam doesn't sell many zero-coupons. But investment houses do synthesize them by purchasing ordinary Treasury bonds, stripping off the semiannual interest payments and using these government promises to pay cash in the future as backing for their own zero-coupon bonds. If you don't get it, don't worry: Synthetic Treasury "strips," which trade on the exchanges, are as good as the real thing.

An easy way to buy zeros is through one of the Benham Target Maturities Trusts (phone 800-472-3389). Each of these six no-load funds (1995, 2000, 2005, 2010, 2015, 2020) owns nothing but zero-coupon Treasury bonds with a single year of maturity. The bonds in the Benham Target 2005 fund, for example, will all mature in 14 years.

The return on the fund is a few-tenths of a percent lower than a direct investment in the zero-coupon bonds. But the convenience—small minimum purchase ($1,000), regular accounting statements, guaranteed liquidity, no broker to bother you—may be worth this modest price.

P.S.: Most zero-coupon bonds (other than those issued by the U. S. Treasury) contain "call" provisions. This gives issuers the right to buy the bonds back at a price specified in advance. Call provisions are never good for bondholders—the right is only exercised, after all, when borrowers feel the deal is working to the advantage of the security owners. But they are an especially rotten deal for zero-coupon bondholders who have purchased the securities in order to lock in the interest rate for a long period.

Actually, the story gets worse. With ordinary bonds, the price at which the bond can be called is always the face value or more. With zero-coupon bonds, the call price is based on a complicated interest-rate formula. And while the information is available to anyone who buys the bond, most buyers—even most brokers—forget to look.

The moral: Don't buy a zero-coupon bond unless you understand how the call provision works. Better yet, don't buy a zero-coupon with a call provision.

BACCALAUREATE BONDS

Most state governments know their citizens are outraged about the rapidly rising cost of tuition and fees at public colleges. But most states also know that their citizens would be even more outraged if they raised taxes in order to roll back college bills. The solution proposed by some dozen states: so-called baccalaureate bonds.

These are nothing more (or less) than zero-coupon, tax-exempt bonds, issued in relatively small denominations and set to mature in time to pay little Elmer's college tuition. The interest rate is generally comparable to other zero-coupon bonds of the same maturity.

Are baccalaureate bonds or other tax-exempt zeros right for you? They make a good set-it-and-forget-it investment, provided that (a) you are in a top tax bracket in a high-tax state and (b) interest rates don't rise sharply between now and the year Elmer is ready to enroll. If your income is less than $60,000, the tax breaks on series EE savings bonds are more attractive (see pages 17–18). And if you are a very conservative investor, look at CollegeSure CDs (see page 20). They are a safer bet, but will probably pay a lower after-tax return.

47

Mortgage-Backed Securities

Once upon a time, banks lent families the money to buy houses. The debt, called a mortgage, remained an asset on the books of the bank until it was paid off. Today many, if not most, home mortgages are sold to investment bankers and government agencies. These financial intermediaries collect a bunch of mortgages—say, $10 million worth—and using them as backing, create "pass-through" securities in wallet-size portions.

Investors who buy these mortgage-backed securities in effect purchase a small slice of several hundred home mortgages. The owners of the securities receive the interest and principal as the home owners pay down (or pay off) their mortgages.

This brave new world of mortgage finance is for the most part a better world, funneling investors' money from Pawtucket or Peoria into new houses in Pittsburgh or Penobscot. As a result, mortgage rates are a little lower and returns to investors in fixed-income securities are a little higher. Very safe mortgage-backed securities pay about 1 percentage point more than Treasury bonds.

The ones issued by the Federal National Mortgage Association (Fannie Maes) and the Federal Home Loan Mortgage Corporation (Freddie Macs) fit the bill. But the most popular mortgage-backed securities for small investors are government-guaranteed securities sold by the Government National Mortgage Association (Ginnie Maes).

Ginnie Maes are initially sold by brokers in $25,000 bites. Thereafter they trade in an active market in much the same way as government bonds. Like bonds, their prices are quoted as percentages of face value: A Ginnie Mae that sells for 80 is selling for 80 percent of $25,000, or $20,000.

If Ginnie Maes are as safe as government bonds and trade as freely, why do they pay more interest? Unlike a bond, the flow of interest and principal is not entirely predictable. Owners receive cash each month, part of which represents principal, part interest. If interest rates fall, more home owners will choose to refinance their mortgages, increasing the flow of principal and reducing the effective term of the Ginnie Mae. But if interest rates rise, relatively little principal will be repaid, and the Ginnie Mae will last longer than the average 12-year life.

Some brokers advertise Ginnie Maes at what seem like impossibly high-interest yields. The catch, rarely explained, is that the securities are selling for more than face value. Thus if the home owners choose to pay off their mortgages quickly (as might be expected), those who own the Ginnie Maes will lose part of their capital.

The moral: *Never buy a mortgage-backed security from a broker with a big smile and a soothing manner. Better yet, never buy a pass-through security directly from anyone.* Buy them from mutual funds, which manage portfolios of mortgage-backed securities on your behalf and have the computers needed to figure the angles on these enticing hybrids. Fund shares, by the way, come in small bites—as little as $1,000.

The following funds are distinguished by low operating costs and competent management:

Benham GNMA Income
800-227-8380
800-982-6150 (CA only)

Dreyfus GNMA
800-782-6620

Fidelity Income—GNMA Portfolio
800-544-6666

Lexington GNMA Income
800-526-0056
201-845-7300

T. Rowe Price GNMA
800-638-5660
301-547-2308

Vanguard Fixed Income – GNMA
800-662-7747
800-362-0530 (PA only)

3

BEATING THE IRS
Tax Shelters That Still Make
Dollars and Sense

Nothing infuriates investors more than giving Uncle Sam part of the hard-won return on their savings. And for good reason. It's true that the maximum federal tax rate on an extra dollar earned has fallen from 70 percent in 1981 to just 33 percent this year. But state and local income taxes add up to 12 percent (Connecticut) to the burden. What's more, inflation raises the effective rate—in some cases to the level of outright confiscation.

Take the sad but all-too-realistic case of an investor who is earning $800 a year (8 percent) on a $10,000 bank CD at a time when inflation is chugging along at a modest 5 percent rate. Let's say our investor is in the 35 percent tax bracket, when both federal and state levies are included. He or she thus owes the tax collectors 35 percent of $800, or $280.

Now for the catch: Of the $800, $500 is phantom income, purchasing power lost to inflation during the year. Just $300 represents a real increase in wealth. So the $280 tax amounts to a whopping 93 percent—not 35 percent—of our hapless investor's real earnings!

That's quite an incentive to seek shelter—any shelter—from the tax storm. But before you get carried away, remember a few key points.

Tax shelter is not an end in itself. What counts is after-tax income. It is always better to pay even a 50 percent tax on $1,000 than to pay no tax at all on $400.

Tax deferral is not the same as tax exemption. Some investments in real estate, for example, permit you to deduct more than you earn in income, postponing the tax liability for years or even decades. But the day of reckoning will come and for anyone who hasn't carefully planned it, the reckoning can be a nasty shock.

Look at the total package, not just the tax consequences. Some tax-sheltered investments are illiquid and cannot be sold in a hurry for anything approaching their true value. And some are very risky—too risky for a middle-income investor with kids to educate and a mortgage to pay off.

Some of the best tax shelters left since the laws were tightened in 1986 are inducements to save for retirement. Read on by all means. But before plunking down your money on the investments outlined below, compare the alternatives in Chapter 4.

Tax-Exempt Bonds

The interest on bonds issued by state and local governments, along with local authorities that run public schools, provide water and sewage services, and so on, is exempt from federal tax. Most states also exempt the interest on bonds issued within their borders. A New York resident pays no tax on bonds issued by, say, the city of Buffalo. But states don't offer such courtesies to each other: A California resident who bought the Buffalo city bonds would be required to pay California income tax on the interest.

Gains from the sale of a tax-exempt bond from any state are taxed as ordinary income. Thus, if you bought bonds this year for $10,000 and sold them next year for $12,000, you would owe taxes on $2,000.

No state or local authority has credit as good as the federal government's, because only the Feds have the authority to honor their debts by printing money. A few states and prosperous cities do have very good credit indeed, earning "triple A" ratings from Moody's and Standard and Poor's bond rating services. But dozens of tax-exempt borrowers do default each year. And assessing this risk is far more difficult for a local government or taxing authority than for a corporation.

With a corporation, bondholders have clear legal claims on the assets of the business. With a local government authority, politics and public ethics muddy the water. If a school district doesn't have enough cash to pay both bond interest and

WHEN TAX-EXEMPT BONDS AREN'T . . .

While all municipal bonds are created equal, since August 1986 some have been created more equal than others. The 1986 tax law defines three classes of state-government sponsored bonds.

Good old "public purpose" bonds, the sort issued directly by government agencies to meet some essential government function, are still fully exempt from federal tax.

"Qualified private activity" bonds, mostly issued to finance low-cost housing and student loans, are also tax-free for most investors. But the interest is considered "tax-preference" income and is thus tossed back into the income pot for purposes of calculating your 21 percent "alternate minimum tax." If you don't know what all this jargon means, it probably doesn't apply to you. And if it doesn't, "qualified private activity" can be a particularly good buy because they generate a slightly higher yield to compensate high-income investors for the partial tax liability.

Some bonds issued by state and local authorities are fully taxable by Uncle Sam because Congress decided the activity being financed does not serve an essential public purpose. Bonds financing sports stadiums and shopping centers fit this category. Note, however, that these bonds are still exempt from home-state taxes, and may be worth owning.

teachers' salaries, who will get the money? Only the judge knows. *Wise investors thus take municipal bond ratings with a grain of salt.*

Like corporate bonds, municipal bonds pay interest twice a year. But unlike corporates, muni's are generally issued in "serial" form. A $10 million dollar bond issue for a school district may thus be sold as a series of twenty $500,000 issues, paying different interest rates and set to mature in sequence over the next 20 years. When a broker speaks of the "8½'s of 2013," he or she means the bonds paying 8½ percent that mature in the year 2013.

Serial form is convenient for the issuer, who wants to pay down a debt gradually. But it reduces the liquidity of individual issues. And it adds to the complexity of picking bonds from a market in which thousands of states, towns, counties, school districts, and myriad financing authorities compete for investors' attention and money.

Tax-exempt bonds are generally sold in multiples of $5,000. But the price of the bond, no matter what its size, is quoted as a percentage of par value. Thus a $5,000 bond selling for 110 is really selling for 110 percent of $5,000, or $5,500. Interest that has accrued on a bond, but has yet to be paid, is tacked onto the selling price.

The best tax-exempt bond brokers are generally the biggest because they maintain a greater variety of bonds in inventory. If you are in the market, try a local office of Merrill Lynch. Or call Lebenthal (800-221-5822, 212-425-6116), the largest specialized municipal bond broker that welcomes retail clients.

Remember, though, that most municipal bonds are traded in wholesale lots of $100,000 or more. Few brokers will be interested in your business unless you are ready to spend at least $25,000 on a single issue. Moreover, the markup on small lots of bonds can be ferocious. If you need to sell a bond quickly, expect to lose 5 or 6 percent of the value.

Does that mean tax-exempt bonds are only suitable for people with a lot of money and a lot of knowledge about the tax-exempt securities market? Not if you are prepared to buy a chunk of a prepackaged lot called a "unit trust," or you are willing to put your trust in a mutual fund.

TABLE 3 ═══════════════════════════════════════

Taxable Equivalent Yields

Single Return 1992
To equal these tax-exempt returns

Your Taxable Income*	Your Tax Bracket	5%	6%	7%	8%	9%	10%
		you would have to earn this return on a taxable investment					
Less than $21,000	15%	5.88	7.06	8.24	9.41	10.59	11.76
$21,000–52,000	28%	6.94	8.33	9.72	11.11	12.50	13.89
$52,000–107,000	33%	7.46	8.96	10.45	11.94	13.43	14.93
$107,000 plus	28%	6.94	8.33	9.72	11.11	12.50	13.89

Joint Return 1992
To equal these tax-exempt returns

Your Taxable Income*	Your Tax Bracket	5%	6%	7%	8%	9%	10%
		you would have to earn this return on a taxable investment					
Less than $36,000	15%	5.88	7.06	8.24	9.41	10.59	11.76
$36,000–86,000	28%	6.94	8.33	9.72	11.11	12.50	13.89
$86,000–178,000	33%	7.46	8.96	10.45	11.94	13.43	14.89
$178,000 plus	28%	6.94	8.33	9.72	11.11	12.50	13.89

*This number is approximate; assumes 5% inflation in 1991

Tax-Exempt Unit Trusts

The unit trust is one of the neatest tricks in the securities book. A big investment banking house buys, say, $100 million dollars worth of muni bonds, spreading the money around a few dozen issues from a few dozen borrowers. It then slices the bonds into $1,000 units and sells them through retail brokers for a 3 or 4 percent commission.

The advantages are obvious. An investor with just a few thousand dollars to spend can own a diversified portfolio of tax-exempt bonds. The bookkeeping is no-muss no-fuss: Payments of interest, plus any principal due, come by monthly or quarterly check.

Moreover, packages of bonds are often tailored to investors' specialized needs. Some unit trusts contain bonds from a single state, relieving residents of the burden of state and local taxes; New York and California trusts abound. But it's not hard to find trusts for other high-tax states, including Massachusetts, Connecticut, New Jersey, Michigan, and Pennsylvania. Some are insured against default by a consortium of giant life insurance companies. Some give you the option of automatic reinvestment of interest in tax-exempt bonds at the prevailing rate. But a few words of caution are in order.

Word one. Sponsors of unit trusts often advertise an average interest rate that is misleadingly high. The payments start at the advertised rate, all right. Soon enough, though, the bonds paying the highest rates are called in by the borrower. And while the owner of the unit trust gets the principal back, the average yield of the remaining bonds is sure to be lower.

Word two. Sponsors of unit trusts typically pledge to buy back units at their market value at any time. But the market value is likely to be lower than the purchase price because the sponsor does not pledge to return the 3 or 4 percent commission. Moreover, the bonds can fall in value if interest rates rise, leaving you with a significant loss of capital. The bottom line: Don't buy a unit trust unless you plan to keep it for four or five years.

Word three. Slices of newly minted unit trusts cost the same wherever you buy them. But unit trusts purchased from the secondary market will cost whatever the broker thinks he or she can get away with. Your only protection is to shop around.

Word four. To goose up the interest rate, sponsors will often lard their unit trusts with bonds from town and authorities with poor credit. As a rule of thumb it makes sense for conservative investors to stick with trusts in which three-quarters of the bonds are rated A or better and none are rated below Baa.

Tax-Exempt Bond Funds

With a unit trust, you own a share in a fixed package of bonds. With a bond mutual fund you own a share of a portfolio of bonds that is managed by an investment company. Which way of owning tax-exempts is better?

Both offer diversification with a minimal investment: As little as $250 gets you in the door at some mutual funds. Both cut the paperwork in owning tax-exempt bonds: Mutual funds will pay out income as dividends or reinvest the money. Both offer liquidity: Mutual fund shares can be redeemed at any time for the market value of the underlying securities.

One real distinction is sales charges. Some mutual funds charge nothing up front to buy shares, while all unit trusts carry a sales "load." Another is management. Unit trust managers function as bookkeepers, distributing income and settling accounts. Mutual funds actively buy and sell bonds in an effort to beat the averages. Such active management is expensive. Added fees can lop one percentage point or more off the fund's income, and there isn't a lot of reason to believe that most fund managers earn their expense-account lunches.

A sensible rule of thumb is buy unit trust if you plan to keep the securities until maturity. If you don't, buy a no-load mutual fund with low operating costs that suits your investment objectives.

High-Grade Funds

Some of these funds limit investments to bonds with very good credit ratings. Others buy insurance against default from a consortium of insurance companies. Either way, conservative investors should be happy.

	Minimum Investment
Financial Tax-Free Income 800-525-8085	$ 250

	Minimum Investment
Safeco Municipal Bond 800-426-6730 206-545-5530	$1,000
SteinRoe Managed Municipals 800-338-2550	$1,000
Vanguard Insured Long Term 800-662-7447 800-362-0530 (PA only)	$3,000

High-Yield Tax-Exempt Funds

These funds trade safety for higher yields. In fact, they don't sacrifice all that much safety; diversification limits the risk the shareholders bear. And in any case, the risks from default are lower with any long-term bond fund than the risks of losing capital as interest rates rise in the economy.

	Minimum Investment
Fidelity High Yield Tax Free 800-544-6666 617-570-7000	$2,500
T. Rowe Price Tax-Free–High Yield 800-638-5660 301-547-2308	$2,500
SteinRoe High Yield Municipals 800-338-2550	$1,000
Vanguard Muni-High Yield 800-662-7447 800-362-0530 (PA only)	$3,000

Limited Term Tax-Exempt Funds

No matter how carefully managed, any bond fund that puts most of its money into bonds that mature 20 years or more down the road is bound to lose value when interest rates rise. *These funds limit this market risk by limiting the terms of the bonds they buy.* Shares are thus less likely to go down when interest rates rise. Remember, however, there is no free lunch here: These funds also earn a little less in interest.

	Minimum Investment
Dreyfus Intermediate Municipal 800-782-6620	$2,500
Fidelity Limited Term Muni 800-544-6666 617-570-7000	$2,500
SteinRoe Intermediate 800-338-2550	$1,000
USAA Tax-Exempt Intermediate 800-531-8181 512-498-8000	$3,000
Vanguard Muni-Intermediate 800-662-7447 800-362-0530 (PA only)	$3,000

Double Tax-Exempt Funds

Residents pay no state or local taxes on these funds because the funds own bonds from a single state (plus Puerto Rico, which are tax-exempt in all states). The yields, however, may be a little lower, reducing the net benefit; before you buy, compare the after-tax yield available from funds that buy bonds in all states.

	Minimum Investment
Dreyfus Funds (CA, MA, NJ, NY) 800-782-6620	$2,500
Fidelity Funds (CA, CT, MA, MI, MN, NJ, NY, OH, PA, TX) 800-544-6666 617-570-7000	$2,500
GIT Funds (AZ, MO, VA) 800-336-3063 703-528-6500	$1,000

Deferred Variable Annuities

Imagine a way to invest in mutual funds without paying a penny of tax on the income until you decide to cash in the investment. Imagine no more: The investment vehicle, confusingly called a deferred variable annuity, is one of the few versatile tax shelters for middle-income investors that survived the tax reform in 1986. Life insurance agents all sell them, as do virtually all "full-service" securities brokers. And many banks, seeking to expand their product lines, are also getting into the act.

Here's how they work. You entrust the money to a life insurance company, either in a lump sum (minimum $5,000) or in occasional, flexible payments (typical minimum $250). The insurance company invests the money as you direct, in anything from a money market fund to a long-term government bond fund to a high-flying common stock fund. The funds are managed by the insurance company itself or by a hired hand—a mutual fund group like Vanguard or Fidelity.

In return for a small service charge, you are generally permitted to switch from one fund to another within the annuity's family of funds. That allows you to adjust your investment to reflect changes in your own willingness to take risks in search of higher returns.

The product is called a "deferred annuity" because the investor has the option of converting the money in the account into an "immediate" annuity—a monthly check, guaranteed by the insurance company for the rest of your life and, if you wish, the life of your spouse. Annuities can be sound investments for retirees who want the security of knowing how much they will have to spend, regardless of how long they live (see page 21). Remember, though, turning your annuity account into an immediate annuity is only an option. Think of deferred annuities primarily as a way to invest in mutual funds.

But we digress. No tax is owed on accumulating income until you withdraw money from the annuity account. At that point, however, the IRS taxes the proceeds as if you were removing income first, then the principal. If, for example, you invested $10,000 initially and accumulated another $15,000 in interest, dividends, and capital gains, the first $15,000 in withdrawals would be taxable at regular income-tax rates. Only then can your principal be removed, tax-free.

All in all, though, deferred annuities can be a pretty good deal. The longer you can defer taxation, compounding pretax rather than after-tax income, the better off you are. Why would anyone invest in mutual funds the old-fashioned way? Several reasons:

• *Penalties for early withdrawals.* Most deferred annuities permit small cash withdrawals each year—typically 10 percent of the principal—without paying a fee. But they usually do exact a 5 to 10 percent penalty on larger sums withdrawn in the first year. Thereafter, the penalty typically declines; most insurers charge no fee at all for withdrawals after the tenth year.

Unfortunately, though, the IRS can be a lot tougher on early withdrawals than the insurance company sponsor. Uncle Sam believes that the only legitimate reason to buy a deferred annuity is to save for retirement. Thus if you make any withdrawals before the age of 59½ (or before you are disabled), you must pay a 10 percent tax over and above any income tax owed.

• *Fund performance.* The mutual funds used by annuity managers have typically performed about as well as the average mutual fund. However, if you happen to choose an insurance company that does not cut the mustard on investment performance, there may be no cheap way out.

• *Administrative fees.* Annuity managers typically charge a flat annual fee of $25 to $30 per annuity, plus 1 percent in "risk charges" to guarantee your beneficiary will collect at least as much as you put in if you die prematurely, plus another ½ to 1½ percent for investment advice. That all adds up to roughly double the fees charged by the typical mutual fund, and could represent quite a drag on the return on your investment. Indeed, if a deferred annuity is held less than 10 years, the extra fees generally more than offset the benefits of deferring taxation.

• *Insurance company strength.* Insurance companies rarely go belly-up. And when they do, policyholders (annuities are, technically, insurance policies) are usually reimbursed from funds set aside by state regulators. Still, it is certainly more prudent to invest with a blue-chip insurance company, provided it offers a competitive product. Before you buy, ask the salesman: Insurers with the deepest pockets are entitled to an A+ rating from the A. M. Best Company.

• *Future tax rates.* The tax rate on withdrawals after age 59½ is the regular income-tax rate. That could work to your advantage—many people end up in a lower tax bracket after retirement. It is possible, however, that your income (or everyone's tax rate) will go up, sticking you with a bigger tax bite later on.

Deferred variable annuities, then, are certainly not recommended for anyone likely to need the money before retirement. The penalties for premature withdrawal and the relatively high administrative fees make deferred annuities a terrible way to save for, say, the kids' orthodonture or a new Lexus. *Nor does it make sense to invest in a deferred annuity before making the maximum possible investment in retirement accounts that provide even better tax breaks.* See Chapter 4 for information on IRAs, SEPs, and 401(k) plans. But deferred annuities can be a pretty good buy for investors with extra cash and very long-term investment goals.

How to pick an annuity? Limit the search to insurance companies with relatively low fees and high ratings for financial strength. The following seven rank high:

Company	Annuity Name	Minimum Investment
Equitable Life	Equivest	$1,000
Fidelity Investments	Fidelity Retirement Reserve	$2,500
General American	IVA	$ 300
Guardian Life	Value Guard II	$3,000
Ohio National	OMNI Plan	$ 250
Prudential	VIP	$1,000
Vanguard Variable Annuity	(direct from Vanguard)	$3,000

Remember that deferred variable annuities are complicated, high-commission products that are often sold by high-pressure agents. Before parting with your cash, comparison shop. For a fee of $10, a company called U. S. Annuities provides the current information on hundreds of annuities. To order a copy of *The Annuity Shopper*, phone 800-872-6684.

THE FIXED ANNUITY OPTION

Deferred variable annuities are all the rage because they offer investors so many choices and generate such terrific commissions for salesmen. But an older and less sexy alternative, the deferred fixed annuity, may still be a better product for investors who do not want to make decisions or to take much risk—yet do want the advantage of tax deferral.

With a fixed annuity, the insurance company offers a single investment option—one that is very close to a certificate of deposit sold by a bank. The interest rate is set in advance for a period as short as three months or as long as five years. Rates typically track the interest on CDs.

Unlike a bank CD, of course, the principal is not insured by the Feds. But as long as the insurance company sponsor stays afloat, your investment is safe. Before investing, ask the salesman whether the insurance company has an A+ rating from A. M. Best, the industry ratings specialist. If it doesn't, shop elsewhere.

The potential pitfalls in investing in fixed annuities are much the same as those associated with flexible annuities. Sponsors usually charge fat fees for early withdrawals, and the IRS looks harshly at any withdrawal before the age of 59½.

Note, too, that the insurance company is not legally bound to offer a competitive interest rate after the initial guarantee expires. Most do anyway. But to protect yourself, insist on a policy with a "bailout provision" permitting you to withdraw cash without penalty should the interest rate fall more than a percentage point or two. In a pinch, this would give you the option of making a tax-free transfer from one insurance company to another.

Banks, savings and loans, securities brokers, and insurance agents all sell fixed annuities. Banks and brokers generally offer slightly better deals than insurance agents because they take smaller commissions. But there is no practical alternative to comparison shopping. A good place to start is with strong insurers known for paying competitive rates on fixed annuities:

Aetna Life	203-273-8920
Nationwide Life	800-848-6331
Metropolitan Life	800-638-5628
USAA Life	800-531-8000

Or buy *The Annuity Shopper* ($10), a rating service that provides basic information on dozens of annuity policies. Phone 800-872-6684.

A last thought. Before buying a deferred fixed annuity, compare the terms to those of a series EE U. S. savings bond (see pages 17–18). The EE bond's interest yield is likely to be somewhat lower. But it is a more flexible investment vehicle: The minimum purchase is smaller, and there are no tax penalties for early redemptions. You may even escape tax entirely if you use the proceeds for your kids' college education.

Cash-Value Life Insurance

Not long ago "ordinary" life insurance was the standard, accepted way of saving for old age. You gave the insurance agent a monthly or quarterly premium check. If you died before age 70, your beneficiaries got the face amount of the policy. If you didn't, you got a big chunk of cash when you retired. And if you needed money in a pinch before retirement, you could always borrow against its accumulated cash value.

It looked like a good deal, and sometimes it was. Uncle Sam was happy to subsidize the enterprise by allowing the cash value to accumulate tax-free until it was withdrawn. *But more often than not, "cash-value" policies were a ripoff.* To begin, the commissions paid to the agent were enormous—typically half the first year's premium and a few percent every year thereafter. If you decided to cancel the policy within a decade of its creation you lost thousands of dollars in savings. Even if you left the policy in force until retirement it usually proved to be a bad deal. The implicit interest rate paid on money accumulating in the policy was typically far below the rate that could be earned safely elsewhere.

PLAIN VANILLA LIFE INSURANCE

When you buy a new sofa, the salesman is unlikely to insist that you also purchase a set of matching lawn chairs. But that, in effect, is what life insurance agents do, packaging your insurance on your life with another financial product—typically a tax-deferred savings or a mutual fund account. For some people in some circumstances it pays to buy the cash-value life insurance package. But for most people who need life insurance, the unbundled form, known as "term" insurance, will do nicely.

Term insurance is simply a bet on your life. If you die during the period the policy is in force, your beneficiaries get the face value of the policy. If you survive, the insurance company owes you nothing.

One of the great virtues of term insurance is that it is fairly easy to comparison shop. The more insurance you purchase, the less it should cost per $1,000 of face value. Pricing on large policies—$250,000 or more—is particularly competitive. But don't get carried away: Buy only as much as you really need. And stick with policies issued by an insurance company that is rated A or better for financial soundness by the A. M. Best Company, the industry's financial rating service. If the agent or the company representative can't or won't tell you the rating, shop somewhere else. It is a jungle out there, and insurance companies do sometimes go broke.

P.S.: If you live in New York, Connecticut, or Massachusetts a good place to start shopping is your neighborhood savings bank. Savings banks generally offer exceptionally good deals on smaller policies.

Today most policyholders experience the same problems: high commissions, poor returns on investment, high penalties for premature cancellation. But careful investors can beat the odds by shopping around.

Is it worth the trouble to try? Probably not: Every advantage of cash-value life insurance can be had more cheaply by combining "term" insurance (see box) with a deferred annuity or series EE savings bonds. But if you insist on trying, start with these companies, all of which keep sales charges to a minimum by selling direct:

Ameritas
800-255-9678

Fidelity Investments
800-544-6666

Lincoln Benefit
800-525-9287

USAA
800-531-8181

For $30 the National Insurance Consumer Organization (703-549-8050) will provide you with a breakdown of the costs of any policy you specify. Write: NICO, 121 North Payne Street, Alexandria, VA 22314.

4

RETIREMENT WITH FRILLS
Living Well Is the Best Revenge

The good news is that Americans are living longer than ever, and are far more likely to stay healthy enough to enjoy it. The bad news is that they are no better prepared financially for a long retirement than they were in the old days, when ketchup was the vegetable of choice and the only reason to walk a mile was for a Camel.

Unless you happen to have spent a lifetime working for some benevolent government agency, your pension plan (including Social Security) is unlikely to cover more than the essentials. But cheer up: The earlier you start saving for retirement the easier it is. What's more, *Uncle Sam makes retirement savings almost painless by offering a slew of tax breaks as incentives.*

This chapter covers the most popular tax-sheltered retirement plans: IRAs, 401(k)'s, Keoghs, and SEPs. Don't forget, though, that more flexible saving vehicles—series EE savings bonds come to mind—can also fit neatly into a retirement strategy. They don't offer comparable tax advantages, but they do give you the option of using the cash before retirement without incurring a tax penalty.

Individual Retirement Accounts (IRAs)

In the golden era of IRAs (1982 through 1986) practically anybody who was employed could sock away $2,000 a year in an IRA account. Taxes on earnings were deferred as long as the money remained in the account. Better yet—far better yet—the annual contribution could be deducted from that year's taxable income. For middle-income folks in, say, the 35 percent tax bracket, that was equivalent to a $350 gift from Washington for every $1,000 they put away for retirement. Then in 1987, tax rates were cut to a maximum of 33 percent. But what Congress gave with its left hand, it took back with the right. Eligibility for the full, up-front tax benefit from IRAs was slashed and taxpayers responded accordingly: Total contributions fell by two-thirds.

President Bush is pressing to restore some (not all) of the tax goodies to IRA savings. And it is conceivable that the new tax breaks will be law by the time you read these words. But don't hold your breath.

If the law isn't changed, does it still make sense to put money into an IRA? Maybe. Much depends on whether you participate in a pension plan, and whether you have a more attractive tax-sheltered alternative for retirement savings— namely, a 401(k) plan. For a more definitive answer, read on.

Eligibility

Anyone with earned income can put money into an IRA. Wages, salary, and self-employment income count as earned; annuities, gifts, pensions, and income on investments do not.

The maximum annual contribution for an individual is $2,000 or 100 percent of earned income, whichever is smaller. For example, someone with a $1,400 part-time job could put away up to $1,400; someone with a full-time job making $30,000 could, at most, stash $2,000. Husbands and wives who both have jobs can set up individual plans, permitting them to contribute a combined total of $4,000. Couples with just one breadwinner are allowed a maximum of $2,250.

Tax Deferral

Once money is in an IRA account, earnings accumulate tax-free until the cash is taken out. That is a nice feature because time is money: The longer taxation is deferred, the more money remains in the account to accumulate interest and dividends. But it is not a benefit that is unique to IRAs and other government-blessed retirement plans. Cash-value life insurance, series EE savings bonds, and deferred annuities also qualify, and such investments offer greater flexibility and require less paperwork. So in itself, tax deferral is not a good enough reason to set up or invest in an IRA.

Tax Deductibility

Now we are talking real money. The ability to deduct an IRA contribution from current income is worth up to $560 annually for an individual in the 28 percent tax bracket (28 percent of $2,000 equals $560, got it?). The catch is that deductibility is restricted.

If you are not eligible for a pension plan at your workplace you may deduct your IRA contribution, no matter how much you make. For those with pension plans, however, deductibility is linked to earnings. Individuals with incomes below $25,000 and couples with incomes below $40,000 may still deduct a full 100 percent of their IRA contributions. On the other hand, individuals with incomes exceeding $35,000 (couples $50,000) get no deduction at all. Those in between the income limits get partial deductions.

The deduction phaseout is proportional to how much you make. For every $100 earned above the $25,000 benchmark, an individual taxpayer making the maximum $2,000 contribution loses $20 in deductions. A schoolteacher with an income of $28,000 would lose $600 in deductions on a $2,000 contribution; he or she would only be able to deduct $1,400.

OK, it's confusing; figuring partial deductibility requires patience—or an accountant. But you don't have to be a rocket scientist to understand the bottom line. If your income is close to the $25,000 (or $40,000) floor you get most of the deduction; if it is close to the $35,000 (or $50,000) ceiling, you get to deduct very little. The definition of income used to measure deductibility, by the way, is the "adjusted gross income" line on your tax return, and thus includes earnings on investments.

Accumulating a Nest Egg

From little IRA acorns do mighty oaks grow: $2,000 invested each year for 30 years in an account that averages an 8 percent return will leave you with almost $245,000 to retire on. That sounds like a lot of money, and it is. But before you book that round-the-world cruise on the *QE2,* remember that a good chunk of spending power of the $245,000 will likely be eroded away by inflation.

How, then, do you calculate the realistic future value of an IRA that accumulates annual contributions over many years? Economists have discovered that interest rates generally rise and fall with inflation rates, on average leaving savers with only enough to stay about 3 percentage points ahead of the game. If inflation averages 4 percent; interest on, say, bank CDs is likely to average about 7 percent. If inflation runs 12 percent, interest rates will be in the ballpark of 15 percent.

Thus to estimate future purchasing power, economists generally assume that the "real" or inflation-adjusted interest rate will run about 3 percent. And $2,000 a year accumulating at 3 percent interest for 30 years would leave about $98,000 in 1992 purchasing power. That's a lot less than $245,000. But the money, bless it, is real, spendable dollars—the kind that will always be able to buy a steak dinner for $25 or a decent car for $10,000.

TABLE 4

Accumulating an IRA Nest Egg

put $2,000 a year in an IRA for:	Earn this much annually:					
	6%	7%	8%	9%	10%	3%
	and you'll retire with					
10 years	$30,000	$31,000	$33,000	$35,000	$37,000	$24,000
20 years	88,000	99,000	112,000	126,000	143,000	55,000
30 years	202,000	245,000	297,000	362,000	442,000	98,000

Setting Up an IRA

The Internal Revenue Service isn't very fussy about where you put your IRA money. Banks, federally insured credit unions, mutual funds, insurance companies, and brokerage houses all qualify as custodians. It is possible to have more than one IRA account or to divide your annual contribution among several accounts, as long as total contributions don't exceed the legal maximum determined by your income. And as far as the IRS is concerned, you are welcome to move an account from one custodian to another.

Nor, for that matter, does the IRS much care how you invest the money. The only no-no's are collectibles (stamps, for example) and tangible assets such as real estate.

THE RULE OF 72

If you've stopped adding money to your IRA account and the balance is earning 7 percent interest, how long will it take to double your money? If the price of a new house is expected to double in 15 years, what is the expected percentage increase in one year?

One way to answer such questions about compound interest is to buy a book of tables, or a pocket calculator made specially for business math. The easy way is to remember the rule of 72.

To figure how long it would take to double your money, just divide 72 by the interest rate. In the case of the IRA, 72 divided by 7 equals 10.3 years. If the average return on the account were 5 percent, doubling would take 14.4 years.

The formula, of course, works just as well backward. If it takes 15 years to double the price of a house, the anticipated annual rate of appreciation must be 72 divided by 15, or 4.8 percent.

But the fact that Uncle Sam is casual about the wheres and whats of IRA investments doesn't mean you should be. Indeed, these could prove to be the most important investment decisions you ever make. For an individual making the maximum contribution over 30 years, the difference between an average 8 percent return and a 9 percent return is more than $50,000. Consider the following major options.

Banks

Banks and savings and loans get the lion's share of IRA money, and for plausible reasons. Most investors want their IRAs to be very safe, and nothing is safer than a bank account insured to $100,000 by the federal government. Banks typically offer IRA investors a choice of money market accounts and CDs of varying terms. Many also offer mutual fund shares—which, it is important to remember, are not federally insured and do fluctuate in value as interest rates and stock prices change.

The big catch with banks is that they often do not give IRA investors the best possible interest rates. *Indeed, for banks, the name of the game is to hook an IRA customer with a terrific deal to start, and then hope that he or she will not be vigilant thereafter.* If you go the bank route, remember to compare rates with other banks before renewing CDs. If your bank pays less than competitive rates, switch custodians. The new custodian, incidentally, is usually happy to do all the paperwork needed to complete the switch. And the transfer is usually costless unless you are required to liquidate a CD before it has matured.

Brokers

The advantage in using a broker as IRA custodian is a broad choice of investments: Most will let you put your money in anything from common stocks to gold bullion. The disadvantage is cost: Most charge $50 to $100 a year to maintain the account on top of hefty commissions to buy and sell the securities within the account.

That makes broker-based IRAs a terrible deal for investors who have yet to accumulate large sums. After all, $100 in fees represents 5 percent of the principal in a $2,000 account. And it remains a questionable deal for almost everyone else, since most of the investment products sold by brokers can be had more cheaply elsewhere.

Insurance Companies

Insurers sell various forms of fixed and variable deferred annuities (see page 58) to IRA investors. Some are well managed and generate competitive returns. But this is particularly treacherous ground for novice investors: The annuities are very aggressively peddled by salesmen whose incomes depend directly on the volume of business. Most annuities, moreover, are very costly to liquidate. If you change your mind and decide to switch to another custodian, you may lose a lot of your nest egg.

Federally Insured Credit Unions

From the perspective of investors they operate like banks, offering money market accounts and insured CDs. If the rates are attractive, the credit union alternative is attractive. But keep in mind the need to compare rates every year or two. The cash you save may be your own.

Mutual Funds

Most mutual funds are happy to serve as custodians for IRAs for modest ($10) annual fees. Most permit switches from fund to fund within the family of funds run by the investment company at nominal ($5) cost. And most waive the minimum investment requirement for IRAs, making it possible to invest as little as $500 in a fund that ordinarily requires a $3,000 to $5,000 initial balance.

That makes them extremely flexible and attractive for IRA investors who want the option of a very safe investment like a money market fund, but may want to switch their investment strategies as their incomes, family responsibilities, and taste for risk change. *The key is to choose a mutual fund group with a broad range of no-load investment alternatives and a policy of holding operating costs to a minimum.* All the following fund groups fit the description.

Dreyfus Service Corp.
800-645-6561
800-782-6620

T. Rowe Price Associates
800-638-5660
301-547-2308

Scudder Fund Distributors
800-225-2470
617-439-4640

Stein Roe and Farnham
800-338-2550

USAA Investment Management
800-531-8181

Vanguard Group
800-662-7447
800-362-0530 (PA only)

SOCIAL SECURITY: STILL NUMBER ONE

Nobody ever lived the high life on a Social Security pension. The expert's rule of thumb is that it takes about 70 percent of preretirement income to maintain living standards into old age. But an individual retiring this year, who was making $50,000, will find that Social Security checks will replace just a quarter of his or her after-tax paycheck. Indeed, probably the only way to make ends meet on Social Security alone is to retire to a foreign country—Poland, Mexico, and Costa Rica come to mind—where the dollar still goes a very long way.

For all but a lucky minority of affluent Americans, however, Social Security does remain the financial bedrock for retirement, the one source that is guaranteed against erosion by inflation. That's why anyone planning retirement should get an accurate reading on how much the government will owe him or her.

To estimate your future benefits—and to make certain you are being credited for past and current payroll taxes—phone the Social Security Administration's toll-free number (800-234-5772). Ask for a copy of Form SSA-7004, Request for Earnings and Benefit Estimate Statement. The agency's computers usually respond within a month with a projection of how much you'll receive if you retire at age 62, 65, or 70.

Rollovers

As noted above, the IRS lets you move an IRA directly from one custodian to another as often as you wish. It also permits once-a-year tax-free "rollovers" in which you actually take possession of money for up to 60 days. Some people use rollovers as backdoor loans; remember, though, *the failure to put the cash back into another IRA within 60 days leaves you liable for incomes taxes, plus penalties* (see below).

A more common use of the tax-free rollover privilege is to divide retirement accounts in a divorce settlement, or to credit a survivor's own IRA with the proceeds from a deceased spouse's retirement benefits.

Withdrawals

Uncle Sam wants you to keep the money in an IRA until you retire. And to make sure you do, he has made it expensive to change your mind. Unless you become disabled, withdrawals before the age of 59½ are subject to a 10 percent penalty tax on top of ordinary income tax.

Wait, there's more to worry about. Uncle Sam also wants to prevent you from using an IRA as a permanent tax dodge in which you leave the proceeds, untaxed, for your heirs to spend. Once you reach age 70½ you must begin to take money out of an IRA. Indeed, you must make a minimum withdrawal that is linked to your own life expectancy and that of your spouse.

The idea here is to get people to draw down their IRAs (and pay ordinary income tax on the proceeds) at a rate that will likely sustain them through retirement years. If for example, you are age 75 and your spouse is 67, you must withdraw at least 5 percent of the money in your IRA(s) during the year.

Money that should be withdrawn, and is not, is taxed at a 50 percent rate. Thus, if you were supposed to withdraw $3,000 and only withdrew $2,000, you would owe a $500 tax on the $1,000 difference. There's no need, of course, to sweat this one until you hit age 70. The tables for calculating minimum withdrawals are published in annual tax guides such as *J. K. Lasser's Your Income Tax* and are also available from the IRS.

401(k) Retirement Plans

Never mind the gobbledygook title. Named after the section of federal law, the 401(k) plan may be the best thing that ever happened to middle-income investors seeking to feather their retirement nests.

If your company has a 401(k) plan, run, do not walk, to the sign-up counter. While the benefits are similar to those enjoyed by IRA investors, the amount that can be tax-deferred is much larger, and the rate of accumulation within the account is often much more rapid because employers kick in a matching share. As with IRAs, the cash accumulated in a 401(k) is yours to keep, even if you leave the employer who runs the plan.

Under the law, payroll deductions for a 401(k) plan are not counted as part of your earnings when it comes times to figure your income tax. The maximum tax-free deduction is $7,000 plus an adjustment for inflation since 1987. This year it will probably run a bit more than $8,800. Taxpayers in the 28 percent bracket who make the maximum contribution of, say, $8,800, will thus save 28 percent of the total, or $2,464, in federal taxes. In addition, they may save another $1,000 or so from the equivalent break on state and local income taxes.

That's only part of the good news. Many employers match part of their employees' contributions—a 50 percent match is typical. They can, however, retain the option of taking back a portion of their matching contribution if you switch jobs within seven years.

Matching programs, incidentally, are not strictly a matter of altruism. Under federal antidiscrimination rules, corporations can't offer generous 401(k) benefits to their senior executives unless employees at the other end of the pecking order are part of the plan. And the match is used to induce junior employees to join.

A participant is legally permitted to make extra contributions to his or her 401(k) plan, provided the total employer-employee contribution does not exceed 25 percent of total salary or $30,000, whichever is less. But this is rarely a good idea. The extra money is not tax-deductible. Thus the only practical benefit to saving this way is that the income on the

---

GIC: WHOSE GUARANTEE?

Now that you've decided to put money into a 401(k) savings plan, one big question remains: Where should you invest the cash?

Most 401(k) plans offer a variety of options—at the very least a money market fund and a long-term fixed-income fund. But the single most popular option these days, an option offered by three out of five plans, is the GIC, or guaranteed investment contract.

GICs are loans to insurance companies, typically for one to five years, at specified rates of interest. Plan trustees like them because they are easy to arrange and require no active management. Plan participants like them because the yield is generally a half percentage point higher than the rate paid on Treasury bonds of the same maturity, and the principal is not subject to fluctuations in value as market interest rates change. And everybody involved likes the sound of that magic word "guaranteed."

To date, GICs have rarely disappointed investors. Just two of the 60 or so insurance companies selling them have failed to pay back the principal with full interest. But it would be unwise to think of GICs as riskless investments. For better or worse, they are simply the unsecured liabilities of insurance company borrowers. And while it is true that most insurance companies have adequate assets to back up their obligations, no one can say with confidence that the industry's faultless record will last indefinitely. Indeed, as competition for 401(k) dollars grows, insurance companies are likely to try to stretch their own earnings by investing in riskier assets.

How to protect yourself? One obvious answer is to put your 401(k) money in something other than a GIC. If you do take the GIC route, keep the term of the contract down to a year or two—the longer the contract, the more time the borrower's credit has to slide. It may also pay to ask the plan sponsor for the insurance company's claim-paying rating. If Standard and Poor's service does not give it a mark of AA or better, invest in something else.

extra money invested accumulates in the account, tax-deferred, until it is withdrawn. And such tax deferral is available in a variety of other, more flexible, investments—notably series EE savings bonds (see pages 17–18) and deferred annuities (see page 58).

Most 401(k) plans offer a handful of investment options, including a money market fund, a common stock mutual fund, and a GIC (guaranteed investment contract), which is like a CD without the federal insurance (see box on page 73). The best investment for you depends on your willingness to bear risk in search of a higher return. Those who are counting on 401(k) cash to enjoy a well-padded retirement would be wise to stick with the more conservative options.

The rules governing withdrawals from 401(k) plans are nearly identical to those for IRAs. Withdrawals before age 59½ are hit with a 10 percent penalty tax, over and above ordinary income tax. The failure to make regular minimum withdrawals after age 70½ is even more severely penalized: Money the IRS thinks should have been withdrawn and wasn't is subject to a 50 percent tax.

But unlike IRAs it is possible to borrow money from a 401(k) without paying a penalty, provided your employer is willing to go along. No more than half the money in the account can be borrowed and the total loan cannot exceed $50,000. The money must be paid back within five years unless it is used to buy a house. Ask your plan manager for the details. In any event, don't use the borrowing privilege lightly. You will be required to pay market-rate interest on the loan, and unlike interest on a mortgage or home-equity loan, it is not tax-deductible. Remember, too, that the point of a 401(k) plan is to accumulate big bucks for a comfortable retirement.

Keogh Plans

Keogh plans are retirement plans for the self-employed. But anyone who has self-employment income—a newspaper reporter, for example, who writes books on the side—can use a Keogh to reduce his or her current tax burden and build retirement savings even if he or she is also eligible for a corporate pension plan.

Keogh plans work pretty much like IRAs, only the paperwork is more complicated and the maximum contributions are much larger. Banks, brokers, mutual funds, and insurance companies can act as trustees; your choice should depend on where you would like to invest the money. Banks generally have the lowest fees, but offer limited investment choices. Brokers offer the widest range of investment products and even give you the discretion to pick individual stock and bonds. But mutual fund companies that operate a large number of funds are often the best bet because they keep fees low, provide investors with lots of choices, and make it cheap and easy to shuffle your portfolio. See the section on IRAs for a list of fund managers that fit the bill.

TABLE 5 ═══════════════════════════════════════

How Many Years Will Your Money Last?

and spent at this annual rate	100,000 invested at this rate:				
	4%	6%	8%	10%	12%
	will last this many years:				
$ 6,000	29	...........indefinitely			
$10,000	14	16	21	...indefinitely	
$14,000	9	10	12	18	indefinitely
$18,000	7	7	8	10	12

Standard, "defined contribution" Keogh plans allow you to put away $30,000 or 20 percent of your self-employment income after business expenses, whichever is less. If, for example, you netted $40,000 from a watch repair business, you could contribute a maximum of $8,000 to your Keogh—and reduce your taxable income by the same amount.

If, however, you are the rare individual who can afford to save (and thereby shelter from taxes) more than 20 percent of income, the way to go is a "defined benefit" plan. With these plans, the maximum contribution is based on an estimate of how much you would need to put away to insure some minimum annual retirement income. This can be tricky stuff; to set up a defined benefit plan you will almost certainly have to pay a pension consultant to do the calculations and justify the size of the contribution.

As with IRAs there are penalties for withdrawing money before age 59½ or for failing to make timely withdrawals after age 70½. But unlike IRAs, the reporting and contribution requirements can be a major downer. To meet the technical requirements of the law, it may actually be necessary to set up two parallel Keogh plans in order to qualify for the full 20 percent maximum contribution. Every plan owner must file a special tax form by July 31 each year, detailing plan assets and contributions. And if your business has employees other than you, you must make provisions for them to participate in the plan.

Is a Keogh plan worth the bother? Compare it with a simplified employee pension plan (see below). But don't let the paperwork alone stop you: The generous tax deductions make up for a multitude of sins.

Simplified Employee Pensions Plans (SEPs)

Problem: You are self-employed and eager to pick up the big tax breaks available through a Keogh plan. But you don't want to put up with the red tape that Keogh plans demand.

Solution: A simplified employee pension plan—SEP, for short. SEPs are really designed for small businesses that want to offer a simple and flexible pension plan for their employees. But they work just as well for businesses with just a single employee—you.

Here's how a SEP works for an individual. You set up a plan through a bank, insurance company, or mutual fund group. And at the same time, you establish a regular individual retirement account (IRA) through the same institution. Each year Uncle Sam allows you to put $30,000 in the IRA or 13.04 percent of your self-employment income, whichever is less. As with a Keogh plan, the contribution is deducted from your income before figuring taxes and no tax is collected on earnings in the account until the money is withdrawn. As with a Keogh plan, the government doesn't much care how you invest the money.

But unlike a Keogh, there is no annual reporting requirement. Once you fill out a single-page form to create the SEP, paperwork is finished for good. And once the IRA account is created, there is no reason to set up a separate account to contribute to an ordinary IRA as well.

Why, then, bother with a Keogh plan? *Keoghs have one significant advantage: They permit you to set aside 20 percent of self-employment income rather than a maximum of 13.04 percent.* Of course, if you cannot afford to set aside more than 13.04 percent, that is no advantage at all.

Mutual fund groups offer the greatest flexibility in investment options and, typically, the lowest fees for SEPs. One of them, Vanguard, charges nothing at all to set up a SEP, and the maintenance costs are very modest. For phone numbers, as well as alternatives to Vanguard, check the list in the section on IRAs above.

One last word: Remember that once money goes into a SEP, there are tough rules about when and how you may take it out. All the rules applying to IRA withdrawals apply to SEP money that is in an IRA account. No loans are permitted from the account. Any withdrawal before age 59½ triggers a 10 percent penalty over and above ordinary income tax. And the failure to make minimum withdrawals after age 70½ triggers a 50 percent penalty tax.

5

INVESTMENTS FOR A RAINY DAY ... OR A HURRICANE
Hedging against Economic Disaster

The Money Manual 1992 is no doom-and-gloom book: Canned peas, freeze-dried Salisbury steaks, and shotgun shells for the fallout shelter just aren't my idea of a prudent investment. But no expert can honestly say there is no chance of an economic crisis—a poorly managed energy shock, a trade war with Japan, an international banking collapse—that cuts the value of stocks by two-thirds and knocks the stuffing out of long-term bonds.

Some of the best hedges against such a disaster are quite familiar. In all but the worst of times, investments in government-guaranteed money market accounts and short-term government securities will float intact on troubled financial waters. Housing—more precisely, the house you live in—fits the category, too. For while housing values could go up or down in a crisis (America has had both experiences in the past 75 years), a house or apartment with no mortgage debt literally guarantees you shelter in the storm. And for many people, this is all the hedge they need or can afford.

But for those who are exceptionally pessimistic or exceptionally conservative about money, other hedges are available. *If carefully planned, insurance against the meanest of eco-*

nomic times can be had for a modest sacrifice in current income.

Gold And Precious Metals

Gold used to be an exceptionally reliable barometer of economic troubles. When nations rattled sabers or inflation reared its ugly head, the price of precious metals went up.

It is no longer so reliable. For one thing, technological improvements in mining have made it economical to recover gold from low-grade ores, dampening the price impact of an increase in demand. For another, the world's two largest producers, South Africa and the Soviet Union, are in the midst of political crisis. The price of gold is now as responsive to expectations about those governments' responses to crisis as it is to expectations about inflation in America.

The prices of other precious metals and diamonds are also marching to the tunes of their own drummers. Much of the demand for platinum, for example, now comes from industrial users who need it for pollution control. Diamond prices depend more on the capacity of the international cartel to prevent cheating than on production or demand. But there is still good reason to believe that in very hard times, precious metals will remain the asset of last resort. If, for example, inflation spiked to 30 percent or the three largest Japanese banks went under, the price of gold would almost certainly skyrocket.

That's why many serious students of investing still suggest that people with $100,000 or more keep 5 to 10 percent of it in precious metals. If you are lucky, the investment will be a small, chronic drag on the overall return of your savings. And if you are unlucky, you won't be nearly as unlucky as the folks who kept all their money in stocks, bonds, and real estate.

There are lots of ways to buy precious metals. Dealers sell newly minted one-ounce gold coins for a few percent more than the underlying value of the metal. Some banks (notably Citibank, phone 800-223-1080) sell gold certificates that represent ownership of bullion stored in vaults. Commodities brokers sell "futures contracts" for gold, platinum, and palladium, which represent the right to buy the metals at a predetermined price a month or a year from today.

But the simplest (and therefore the recommended) way to

buy gold is through mutual funds that can own both bullion and gold mining stocks. The following funds charge no load and keep ongoing expenses within reason.

	Minimum Investment
Benham Gold Equities Index Fund 800-227-8380 800-982-6150	$1,000
Lexington Goldfund 800-526-0056 201-845-7300	$1,000
USAA Investment Trust—Gold 800-531-8181	$1,000
Vanguard Special Portfolio—Gold 800-662-7447 800-362-0530 (1 percent redemption fee, but very low management fees)	$3,000

Foreign Currency

Different disasters call for different hedges. In one scenario, America fails to pull up its socks on the federal budget deficit. German and Japanese savers, fearing dollars will evaporate in inflation, decide to park their cash somewhere else. As a result, the exchange value of the dollar falls sharply with respect to the currencies of other industrialized nations.

If you find this scenario plausible—and in the closing months of 1990 it looked pretty good—the right hedge is foreign currency. The classic foreign currency hedge is in the organized financial futures market, where corporations doing business abroad lock in the price they will pay for the currency they need months down the road. An investor with $10,000 to $20,000 could play the hedging game with them, buying futures contracts through a commodities broker. But both expertise and care are needed to do it right; and this is no place for a tutorial.

Foreign Currency Bank Accounts

Citibank in New York is pioneering a more convenient way to build a stake in foreign currency: the insured foreign currency account. Dollars put into one of these accounts are exchanged into the foreign currency of your choice—British pounds, for example—and then invested in short-term money market securities. Any time you wish, you may cash in the currency (including interest earned) for dollars at the prevailing exchange rate. The holdings in the account (but not the exchange value back into dollars) are guaranteed, like any other bank deposit, by the Federal Deposit Insurance Corporation.

For the moment, however, the minimum deposit required by Citibank is $50,000, far more than the average investor can afford. That suits Citibank, which is targeting affluent depositors only. But if the accounts catch on, other banks will probably come into the market with smaller minimums.

Foreign Currency Money Market Funds

These funds go after super-high yields by investing in short-term securities from Australia, Britain, Canada, and other countries with high interest rates. Thus far they've done very well, beating the best dollar-based funds by as much as 5 percentage points annually.

If this sounds too good to be true, you have a good ear. Investments in foreign currencies—particularly these foreign currencies—are risky because exchange values are apt to change rapidly. These funds all take some precautions against exchange losses, using fancy financial hedging techniques to minimize the risk of loss. But they are of limited use as a hedge against a fall in the dollar because they do not invest in strong currencies like the Japanese yen and the German mark that will perform best when the dollar goes down. If you do invest, expect to pay a small load.

Alliance Short Term Multi-Market Trust
800-221-5672
201-319-4000

Merrill Lynch Short-Term Global Income Fund
800-637-3863
609-282-2800

Shearson Lehman Short-Term World Income Fund
212-528-2744
(or any local SL office)

Foreign Currency Bonds

Big corporations (like Royal Dutch Petroleum) and foreign government agencies (like the French toll road authority) issue bonds that can be purchased through any large full-service broker in America. You can buy these bonds with dollars. But the interest and principal are denominated in foreign currency, and bond values fluctuate with the rate of exchange. If the dollar falls, you will probably get back a lot more than you put in.

German marks and Swiss francs are the currencies most popular with investors who want to bet against the dollar. But bonds denominated in "ecu's" (short for European Currency Units, an index of all major European currencies) represent a purer hedge against dollar depreciation. Whichever currency you choose, stick with bonds that carry a AAA rating; these are typically bonds backed by stable European governments or by the bluest of blue-chip corporations.

The big disadvantage of using bonds to hedge against the dollar is the high cost of buying or selling. This market is built to serve very large institutional investors who trade bonds by the million. Smaller investors with only $10,000 to $20,000 invariably pay markups of 4 or 5 percent—markups that cannot be recovered when you sell. Remember, too, that foreign currency bonds, like any long-term fixed-return investment, fluctuate in value with interest rates. You thus might make money when the dollar falls, only to lose it again when interest rates rise.

The cheaper way to buy small quantities of foreign currency bonds is through a mutual fund. Funds offer wholesale buying power to retail customers. They can also muster the expertise to pick and choose among lower-rated bonds paying higher interest rates.

Unfortunately, most foreign bond funds are peddled as a way of earning exceptionally high current yields rather than as a hedge against the dollar. They are thus obliged to invest in currencies like the Australian dollar, whose bonds pay high yields but aren't as likely to go up in value in tandem with strong European currencies. Still, they do offer some currency exchange protection and will likely provide more in coming years as fund managers scramble to match the gains offered by European currencies in a time of a weakening dollar. The following funds charge no load and don't burn a lot of the income on fees:

	Minimum Investment
Fidelity Global Bond 800-544-6666	$1,000
T. Rowe Price International Bond 800-638-5660 301-547-2308	$2,500

The following are "closed-end" international bond funds, whose shares can be purchased through any securities broker. Read the section on closed-end funds (page 38) before investing.

Global Government Plus
Global Yield Fund
Templeton Global Income Fund

6

PUTTING IT ALL TOGETHER
Sample Investment Strategies

You are unique: The right investment strategy for you is not the right investment strategy for the yuppie lawyers who just renovated the Victorian down the block, or your cousin Harry, who was finally promoted to manager for the letter "R" at the local encyclopedia publisher. But these sample strategies should still be helpful in figuring out where to put your money.

I. Just Starting Out

You are single, age 28, and earn $26,000 in a job that promises rapid promotion. Deductions for taxes and the major medical plan leave you with $1,600 to spend each month. Your parents can take care of themselves financially. In fact, it's all you can do to stop Mom from enclosing $250 checks in every letter she sends. Your one-bedroom garden apartment is a little small, and the communal swimming pool could use a face-lift. But with rent of only $450 a month and your long-term plans up in the air, you see no reason to scrimp to carry a mortgage.

You have no debts except for the $3,000 still owed on a 1990 Camry. And you've accumulated $12,000 in savings. You figure you could save about $300 a month if you were really motivated.

RECOMMENDED PORTFOLIO
Local bank checking/money market account	$4,000
One-year bank CD	$5,000
Nicholas II Fund	$3,000

401(k) plan	$2,000
Nicholas II Fund	$1,000

Comments: A money market fund or a money market account in another city would pay an extra percentage point in interest. But the loss is more than made up by the savings on checking charges, credit card fees, and car loan interest at a local bank that is offering a package deal. On the other hand, it makes sense to shop for the highest-yielding CD; the difference could be $100 a year—not much, perhaps, but enough for a couple nights out or a dozen new tapes for the car stereo.

It may seem premature for a 28-year-old to put almost 8 percent of his or her income into a 401(k) plan. But the immediate tax savings—our single taxpayer is in the 28 percent federal bracket—is nothing to sneeze at. And the company is offering an irresistible dollar-for-dollar match in order to encourage midlevel employees to participate.

The Nicholas II Fund is a growth-oriented no-load mutual fund with an excellent track record. It could easily have a bad year or two and is almost certain to suffer the occasional losing quarter. But our 28-year-old can afford to take a few chances. And the fund offers an excellent way to test his or her responses to investment risk before the results matter very much. Note that only one fund is recommended; there just isn't enough money at stake to bother with further diversification.

II. Two Incomes, Good Prospects, Greater Ambitions

You are married (ages 33 and 27), and you both have college degrees and good jobs. Your combined income is $80,000; with any luck it will hit six figures in the next two or three years. Generous company pension plans have been building equity for retirement. Your take-home pay is $4,800 a month, which hardly seems enough to cover the $1,500 mortgage payment on the $170,000 house you bought three years ago after you finally paid off the college loans.

That mortgage, thank goodness, is your only debt; both the four-year-old Jeep and the six-year-old Camaro are owned free and clear. But you have only $6,000 in liquid savings. You are determined to start accumulating cash for kids and, if everything goes just right, a time-sharing ski condo at Winter Park. Your monthly savings goal: $700.

Checking accounts	$6,000

RECOMMENDED ANNUAL SAVINGS STRATEGY

Dreyfus Worldwide Dollar Fund	$2,500
One-year bank CD	$2,000
Vanguard S&P 500 Index Fund	$2,000

Comments: This family is cash-poor and maybe a little house-poor, too. They barely have enough money on hand to cover the monthly ebb and flow of bills—not to mention minor emergencies like a new transmission for the Camaro. But $700 a month savings (a lot for a couple with $4,800 to spend each month) will build a financial cushion in a hurry.

The Dreyfus Worldwide Dollar Fund consistently pays a half percentage point more than the average money market fund, with no loss in safety. A few other funds pay as much, but require larger initial investments. A bank CD in the highest-yielding bank available may seem an unexciting place to invest. But this couple needs to build some security before moving on to riskier investments. Besides, if history is any indication, the money going into the Vanguard stock index fund will outperform two out of three stock mutual funds.

III. And Baby Makes Three

You are married (ages 36 and 32), both working and expecting a first child. Your combined income is $55,000, which will fall for a year or two while Mom figures out a more flexible working arrangement with her employer. Luckily, there is a terrific day-care center a half-mile away that only costs an arm and a leg. The take-home from the $55,000 comes to $3,400 a month.

Your first order of business is living space. You are getting by in a two-bedroom apartment, which will become a claustrophobic nightmare once junior begins to crawl. House prices, which had been going up more rapidly than your income, have finally leveled off. You expect to put down $25,000 of your $35,000 in savings on a $120,000 house. And once the dust settles, you hope to put away another $400 a month in savings.

RECOMMENDED PORTFOLIO

Checking account	$ 5,000
Scudder Short Term Bond Fund	$30,000

    One-year bank CD $ 2,000
    Series EE savings bonds $ 2,500

Comments: A good money market fund—Dreyfus Worldwide Dollar or Vanguard Money Market Reserves Prime Portfolio—would be good places to park the cash that's needed in the next year or two for the down payment. But the Scudder Short Term Bond Fund is an attractive alternative. The money is accessible without penalty on short notice. And the shares should return a somewhat higher yield than a money market fund without putting the principal at more than minor risk.

Once they've bought a house, this family's first objective will be to rebuild its liquid assets. Some savings could be funneled into the Scudder fund; or, if the interest rate on one-year CDs look considerably better (as they have in recent months), they could shop for the higher yield.

Held for five years or more, the series EE bonds are a very competitive way to save. And they offer a double whammy: If this family's income does not grow much faster than inflation, the interest from the bonds could be used, tax-free, to pay junior's college bills.

IV. Coping with Tuition

You are widowed, age 42, and left with a 10-year-old to bring up alone. Luckily, life insurance paid off the mortgage and left you with $100,000 in cash. You've hung onto a good job, and, combined with Social Security survivor's benefits, you're bringing home $3,500 a month. But there's no pension plan where you work. Your first priorities are guaranteeing little Alicia's college tuition and building funds for retirement.

RECOMMENDED PORTFOLIO
    Checking/bank money market account $20,000
    CollegeSure CD $60,000
    Fidelity Spartan Market Index Fund $20,000

RECOMMENDED ANNUAL SAVINGS STRATEGY
    Individual retirement account
        Vanguard Fund Group $ 2,000
    Series EE savings bonds $ 2,000

Comments: The local bank offers those willing to keep $20,000 on hand a great package deal on checking and money market services. But it's worth keeping an eye on the interest rate; should the bank let it fall a percentage point below the best money market funds, make the switch.

The $60,000 CollegeSure CD is an inflation-proof way to cover all the cost of a four-year education at a good state school, or most of the cost at a private college. Note, though, that a few thousand dollars in taxes will have to be paid each year on the interest accumulating in the CD.

Anyone with this much money and long-term savings goals should have a stake in the stock market. The Fidelity Spartan Market Index Fund (or the equivalent Vanguard fund) is a good, low-cost way to keep a hand in stocks.

The IRA is a must, providing both immediate tax advantages and income for retirement. Keep open the options on how to invest the IRA money by parking it in a good mutual fund group like Vanguard.

Boring old series EE savings bonds are an extremely versatile investment. If our widow's income remains in the current range, she can use the proceeds, tax-free, to help pay Alicia's tuition; if her income tops the range where the tax break is available, the bonds can be left to accumulate interest, tax-deferred, until retirement.

V. Eyes on Retirement

You are both 52; the house and the three-year-old Saab are paid for, and the kids are on their own. You are making a solid $85,000 a year, and have $20,000 in the bank. But apart from Social Security and the company's anemic pension plan, you just haven't gotten around to accumulating capital for a comfy retirement. You figure that, after taxes and expenses, you can put away $15,000 a year.

RECOMMENDED INVESTMENT
Checking account	$ 5.000
Vanguard Money Market Reserves	$15,000

RECOMMENDED ANNUAL SAVINGS STRATEGY
Two-year bank CD	$ 5,000
SteinRoe Managed Municipals	$ 4,000
Dodge and Cox Balanced Fund	$ 2,000
Janus Venture Fund	$ 2,000
Ivy International Fund	$ 2,000

Comments: $5,000 a year in medium-term bank CDs will rapidly build an ultrasafe cash base. This family's high income makes tax-exempt bonds a pretty good investment too, and the SteinRoe fund has an excellent record for beating the bond yield averages.

The rest of the savings, 40 percent of the total, will grow very rapidly if the economy does well; and our family's capital will probably remain intact even if it doesn't.

The conservatively managed Dodge and Cox Balanced Fund has outperformed the average stock fund in recent years, and would almost certainly do better than average if the stock market turned sour. The Janus Venture Fund, a higher-risk/higher-return fund, invests primarily in smaller companies; the initial minimum investment is $4,000, but Janus Venture permits smaller investments thereafter. The Ivy International Fund provides a stake in European and Asian stocks, and offers some protection against a fall in the exchange value of the dollar.

VI. Lobster on a Fish-Sticks Pension

You're a healthy 67 and 65, and ready to enjoy some leisure after four decades in the white-collar salt mines. Experts believe it takes 70 to 80 percent of preretirement income to maintain living standards in retirement. But Social Security and one corporate pension won't replace more than half your $60,000 earnings. Happily, though, you've thought ahead. You've stashed $70,000 in a corporate 401(k) savings plan, plus another $30,000 in an IRA. And by trading down from your six-bedroom suburban establishment to a two-bedroom condo, you've managed to raise another $200,000.

RECOMMENDED INVESTMENT

Checking account	$ 5,000
Kemper Money Market Fund	$ 15,000
Immediate annuity	$200,000
Vanguard Fixed Income-GNMA	$ 50,000
Lexington Goldfund	$ 10,000
Dreyfus Peoples Index Fund	$ 20,000

RECOMMENDED SAVINGS

One-year bank CD	$ 5,000

Comments: The cash in the 401(k) plan and the IRA can be "rolled over" tax-free into an immediate annuity sold by an insurance company. Add another $100,000 to the annuity and you have enough capital to guarantee about $2,000 a month in income for the life of both husband and wife. The Vanguard

GNMA fund will generate a lot of income, too—perhaps $400 a month.

A small investment in gold (the Lexington Goldfund) represents an insurance policy against hard economic times. A slightly larger investment in a stock index fund gives this couple a way to benefit from continuing economic prosperity.

It may, on first glance, seem odd for retirees to squirrel away almost 10 percent of their income. If this couple doesn't keep saving, though, the purchasing power of their income will be eroded by inflation. And even 5 percent inflation for a decade would be enough to reduce our lobster gourmands to a fish-stick diet.